The Soul's Plan & Purpose

Elliott Eli Jackson

Publications by

Elliott Eli Jackson

Cacophony
From God to You: Absolute Truth
The Sapiential Discourses Universal Wisdom
The Sapiential Discourses Universal Wisdom, Book II
The Sapiential Discourses Universal Wisdom, Book III
The I AM Mantras
The Sapiential Discourses Study Workbook Series

Publications by

Elliott & Diane Jackson

365 Days with Source
I Know Where God Is
I AM Beautiful

The Soul's Plan & Purpose

All There Is, Was, and Ever Shall Be
through Elliott Eli Jackson

Photographs, Digital and cover Images,
Pixabay - https://pixabay.com, 1/12/2019

Copyright © 2019 by Elliott Eli Jackson
All Rights Reserved.

No part of this book may be used or reproduced in any manner without prior written permission from the publisher, except in the case of brief quotations embodied in critical reviews and articles.

The scanning, uploading, and distribution of this text via the Internet or via any other means without the permission of the publisher is illegal and punishable by law. Please purchase only authorized electronic editions, and do not participate in or encourage electronic piracy of copyrighted materials. Your support of the author's rights is appreciated.

ISBN: 9781793989116

Imprint: Independently published

CONTENTS

Dedication
Acknowledgements
Preface
Introduction The Soul's Plan & Purpose

1. Your Plan
2. Elliott's Original Map & Life
3. Diane's Original Map & Life
4. Patricia's Original Map & Life
5. Amy's Original Map & Life
6. Beverly's Original Map & Life
7. Eric's Original Map & Life
8. Erin's Original Map & Life
9. Billy's Original Map & Life
10. Examples of Some Other Life Plans
11. How to Find Your Life Plan & Map

Dedication

This book is set forth for all of you. Each person on Earth has a plan. Yes, believe it or not. And your plan is a most glorious one. It is yours and yours alone. Further, each of you matters in the grand scheme of things. Your goal is to remember this.

Acknowledgements

As always I must thank Diane for the editing work on this manuscript. There are six individuals that Source has requested to provide contributing chapters. They are but a mere representation of the millions on planet Earth that have come to understand, on a deeper level, their Soul Plans and some of their Purposes, and have made giant strides towards fulfilling them. They are Patricia Zimmerman, Beverly McCaw, Amy Barry, Erin Kelly, Eric Watrous, and Billy Rapka. Diane, I and SOURCE/God wish to acknowledge and thank them for their offerings and for allowing others to have a glimpse into their past, and their now, which leads into their future. We also thank them for their courage and perseverance. Their writings will touch millions.

The Journey

The Journey of a soul is long.
The Journey is hard at times.
Its way twists and turns, and is arduous,
audacious.
The Journey is continuous
and sometimes religious.
Religious in the fact that there are no breaks.
Along the way there is no resting place.
The Journey may slow down from time to time,
Yet not for very long.
Fore, the Journey must go on.
The struggles in your life must be born.
They must grow, then they must die,
If in fact one is to fly,
Fly to the heights of self to become one's best
at the end of the Journey.
Fore, remember, the heights have already been
set.

Preface

This book is the result of many across the globe asking for more information on the Soul Purpose or Plan. In *The Sapiential Discourses Universal Wisdom*, Book III, Source sets forth a chapter on the Soul Purpose. However, more and more of you have been asking, seeking and praying for more information of the subject, because more of you are ready. Therefore, since Source always answers prayers, new information is available. Now, some of the information in this book is a reprint directly from Book III. Yet, still, Source has added more information and insight on the Soul Purpose or Plan. Source lets us know what it is and what it is not. Source desires for all of us to get it right, so to speak, in the life that we are living so we won't have to endure another life on Earth. That is, of course, unless we desire to do so. So, down much deeper into the rabbit hole of the Soul Plan we go. Deeper and deeper into the complexities and intricacies of your life on Earth we go.

The constant reminder: This entire book, except for the preface, dedication, acknowledgements, poetry, and the chapters written by six others, was originally typed by All There Is, Was, and Ever Shall Be – Source/God – through the physical being of Elliott Eli Jackson while he was in an unconscious state of being.

Many of the words and phrases that follow within this text are bolded for implantation and remembrance processes. The remembrances will be occurring on a subconscious level within you, the reader. It is a subliminal effort by US, All There is, Was, and Ever Shall Be.

The Parterre of My Life

The past is but a Parterre.
All the days lie in-between
The emotions of my being.
It's as if the orchestra of the universe
Is behind me pushing my endeavors.
The populist of my thoughts
Drive me day and night.
I've been smuggling the events of my life
In the darkness.
Yet, they are indeed in concert with everything.
I do not feel as if that is true.

If any angle was not correct, I cannot tell.
I continue to march to the sound of my soul.
I continue to walk the Parterre of my life,
In and out of situations and events,
Reminding myself that all is as it should be,
Not as it could be.
Therefore, the garden of my soul is watered,
Nourished, and overseen by the spirit.
I am well.
I am, yes, where I should be.

I am not roaming rampant
Throughout the masses of the earth.
My walk is guided,
The path is steady,
The course is fixed.
I am well on my way to Nirvana.

Introduction The Soul's Plan & Purpose

WE, the collective, in OUR infinite wisdom, decided to expand and expose more information on the Soul's Purpose or Plan. There are still far too many of you who do not think you belong on Earth or think that you have not reason and purpose. Now this line of thinking could not be further from the truth. Each of you has reason and purpose. Each of you have rhyme and reason for being. Each of you are wonderful, glorious, and have tasks to do for yourself and for your others.

Far too many of you still question your reason for being. It should not be this way. Each of you are loved more than you can comprehend. Each of you matter to US and to many others. Your decisions do matter, and they affect more than just yourself. Your life does not have be hard and tedious. However, the trick to making your life better is up to you and only you. No other on your planet can make you happy. Now, they can accentuate your life and give you a better understanding of your place and who you are. Yet they cannot and must not define you. It is with this that WE provide the following information. Some of the information is new, as you understand the term. Moreover, most of it has been stated throughout time on your home, your planet your Earth. Many of you only have not been listening or not seeking in the right place or places as you understand those terms.

So, please, WE beseech you, WE implore you to study the following and take heed for it is all true.

Due to the nature of this book there will be many who obtain and read it that have not read OUR previous offerings through Elliott. It is advisable to do so to understand all the important information that WE, Source/God has sent your species. Yet if you have not, WE will provide here all the information necessary for you to fully grasp what happens after death. Fore, it is crucial, and a key to understanding the process that a Soul takes to formulates its new **Life Plan** before it takes human form. Because all things are connected, this information will assist one in obtaining more clarity and a better comprehension of the Soul's Purpose or Purposes. It will also give more insight into exactly how certain choices are made in deciding the parameters or forming factors in a Soul or Life Plan and the following of the **Life Map. Now each Life Map holds within its structure the Purpose or Purposes of a being**. And, better still, the reader will be able to see how choices and decisions can change or alter a Life Plan and Life Map. However, take note that the Life Purpose or Purposes never really Change. They can be altered, and they may not be completed. The non-completion of such can and most often will result in another lifetime. Now, WE offer a quick refresher on what occurs at death, as you understand the term.

At Death

After WE, the very air, leaves an encasement, the soul or spirit travels through the **Tunnel of Life or Lives**. If and after the soul or spirit breaches the three-quarter point of the Tunnel of Life, it will not return to the body and must proceed because it has:

- Decided to leave totally.

- Completed all tasks it chose to do in the physical life it is leaving.

Therefore, it continues to the **Library of Souls**! When the soul or spirit enters the Library of Souls, it is greeted by nothing and no one. The spirit automatically goes to its book of lives (which is a collection of books) that is kept and housed within the library. **All spirits** on all planes of existences **have a book of lives**. Therefore, the number of books are countless. Each book or collection is a **Tondaus** (massive numbers, symbols, signs, notations, grids, and non-custodial nomenclature graphs and schematically set blueprints) of the life just left and the lives lived by a soul or spirit throughout time, as you understand that term. The book is really a historical holographic picture of all lives lived by the soul or spirit. Additionally, the book is seven-dimensional in form and shape. Each book holds within its pages panoramic images of all encasements, whatever they may have been, that a soul or spirit experienced. The book includes abortions or non-births that a spirit chose to experience in a short lifetime. However, not included are **abortions or non-births experienced through a body that were not the choice of the being but were the choice of the child that did not come.** The book is very graphic and artistic in its nature and presentation. This is to say, it holds all manner of actions, decisions, behaviors, reactions, counter-actions, mis-takes, victories, triumphs, and failures of a soul or spirit. The soul or spirit intuitively knows which chapter to go to for the necessary information. The soul or spirit **never** reads a book in its collection that is related to previous forms of life that were prior to the lifetime just experienced. There is no universal reason for it to!

Note: There are those on your planet and others that are granted and contracted to read small portions of the information housed there to assist others in raising their personal vibration. You have named them **Readers of Akashic Records**. Those individuals must maintain a high level of vibration. If those on your planet and others whom have this gift do not maintain self, the entrance is revoked or denied. So please make sure that those who you may seek out for information held in the library are at a high vibration. If they are not, you would not be receiving accurate information.

If a Spirit returns to US after a Lifetime

During the soul's or spirit's review of the life that it lived, it discerns if, in fact, it did accept everything and everyone (all souls and spirits) as equal and treated them as such in the life just lived. If the review affirms that the spirit or soul did such, it will not have to automatically experience another lifetime. Thus, the soul or spirit has the option to return to US, the Oneness. This return, however, is after a few additional stops that are necessary on its way back to from whence it came. One would be the Andromeda Plane (Ascension Plane). This is the plane closest to the Oneness in relation to time, space and distance. This plane's focus is always on beauty. A soul or spirit has the option to remain there for one plank length of time to immerse itself in beauty abound. Further, a soul or spirit has a choice to go to the Conceptis Plane to ponder over, debate, and/or review any and all universal ideas and concepts with other spirits on and in this plane. Souls or spirits there also review the progress of all planets and discuss what avenues are available and appropriate to assist any planet that has fallen behind in its evolutionary process. If the spirit, while on the Conceptis, desires and/or wishes to sojourn to said planet to assist it, it may do so. Additionally, the sending of technical information and/or spiritual revelations are decided for planets in need of such. After a soul or spirit has done that which it needed to do on this plane, for a time period that you would not understand right now, it will return to US in totality.

Once with US, the soul or spirit will petition self to determine if it should return in some kind of encasement on your planet or any other to assist the other encasements of such planet in its evolution process. The spirit or soul, if it chooses such, will go to and through the Sculptor Plane to acquire or obtain its new numerical calibrations. The soul or spirit will also receive the nature of the next encasement. Additionally, it will be given its quantitative quantum analysis mold and universal permission to become the next encasement it has chosen. After such, it will be reincarnated into an embryo in the mother and on or in the place of its choosing. These kinds of lifetimes will always be as a master, teacher, healer, or in some kind of encasement that is not like the majority of dwellers on such planet, i.e., in a grouping that is having or receiving great difficulty with being accepted and treated as equal on such planet. Their return to an encasement form will be only to assist the inhabitants of a planet with compassion, tolerance, patience, acceptance, and truths. Now, because of the vast number of souls and spirits in the winds of time, the number that choose to return is small as compared to the number of souls or spirits that choose to stay in the Oneness.

>If the soul or spirit does not return to US
>it will begin to form its Life or Soul Plan.

Soul Plans are simple, believe it or not. Within this book WE, Source/God, will be placing prior to each person whom WE have requested to contribute to this book their personal **original** Life Map. Now, once again the Life Map holds within it the Life Purpose or Purposes of the person. Additionally, **the Life Map is what should occur in one's life, yet not what necessarily occurs.**

Furthermore, the Life Map is not always in sync with the **Age Markers** which WE will also be presenting to you within this text. WE have had Elliott inform each person of the placement of their Maps before their writings. Most, if not all, of them were taken aback to say the least. Each first thought was "I don't wish people to know or see how far I may have ventured from what I was or are supposed to do. Yet WE did have Diane and Elliott calm their beings. Therefore, you the reader will be able to track and compare their original map with some of the actual events in their lives. You will be able to see, through what they share, how many original parts of their map which include their Purpose or Purposes were either – **Deterred, Delayed, Altered, Completed or In Progress,** or if they even happened, all due to their choices. You will be able to see deviations in their lives which affected their map and the completion of their Purpose or Purposes. Therefore, you should be able to discern how decisions by them altered said Plan or Map and how far each went astray from the original Plan or Map. Further, you will be able to see how they view their lives versus what was on the original map.

It is important for the reader to know that deviations were OK, as you understand the term, for everyone is back on track to fulfill their plan. This is good news for all of you because each of you is exactly where you need to be in your plan due to freedom of choice being your greatest gift. Additionally, each of you can change, at any given moment, and return to your original plan. Yet the **altering** of one's plan can affect the Purpose or Purposes of the being realized or fulfilled.

Once again, all soul plans are SIMPLE. On your planet and all others, all creatures, whatever the makeup, sometimes in the lifetime that is being lived, ask this question. **What is my purpose?** And you well should. Therefore, when you think or ask it of US or anyone else on your planet, do not think it odd or out of place. It is natural. It is innate to desire to know why you are alive or living. WE have placed these very thoughts within the minds of all of you on Earth and everywhere else, the notion of what is my Soul Plan or Purpose. Now on your planet and others, there are many speaking about and writing about such. On Earth, some of the information that is written about is on point. This is because WE have given, through high vibrational Angels, the information on this subject. This information should be disseminated across your planet. So please investigate such; it is important. WE requested that the Angels begin to whisper information about the plan of the soul to more of you in dream and awake time. Why? Because it is a fact of the universes, as you understand the term. There is a Soul Plan. Each and every, soul/spirit on Earth, which includes yours, does have a Soul Plan or Purpose. However, it is not, ofttimes, as you may think or have been told. Fore, it is simple. **Remember**, all spiritual things are simple. Yes, it is most defiantly the mind influenced by lower portions of US that complicate and convolute.

Each lifetime that you have lived or may live has had or has purpose, purposes and reason. **Yet it is important to understand that this is not – Predestination** (control that WE/Source/God may exercise over one of you). WE do not do such. This would infringe on freedom of choice. WE fully understand that most of you have or may have been told this, yet it is simply not true. Or you may have come to believe that all events have been or are the will of Source/God/US. This is true, to a certain extent, **only to the point** that through a person's freedom of choice, all things become OUR will. Fore, OUR will is for you to do that which you desire to do and nothing else, which is:

1. Have freedom of choice.

2. Return to US/WE/God/Source.

Furthermore, and forevermore, there is not fate or destiny, as you understand those words. Well then, you should ask, what is there? Of course, WE will let you know. WE always do.

However, and additionally, **all souls or spirits will return to US** from whence they came. And the ultimate returning to US is contingent upon a Soul completing its Purpose or Purposes. Yes, a beings Purpose or Purposes is set, but it does not fall under the definition of predestination but under Freedom of Choice. So, now, outside of that, which WE just mentioned (set Purpose or Purposes, WE have no control or say. Of course, WE could, fore, there is nothing that WE can't do. WE just do not and will never desire to control any of you. That would be boring to US in totality. A life, your life, is by design to be lived by one of you and only you. It is your life. Your life is not – experienced by US in totality. It is experienced by US through you. Further, it is stated that WE are Sovereign, but WE are not that either. First, WE are not and will never fall under the description of a king, queen, dictator, or any kind of supreme ruler. **WE do not rule.** WE do loving observance with some assistance through your angels, and sometimes a soft or heavy nudge from US. Further,

WE do not have subjects, nor do WE desire any. Nothing that any of you do is or has been decided by US, except for the two things that WE mentioned.

God's Will ~ My Will

Say what Bill,
God's will is my will?
What does that mean?
Cause I do what I do when I want to do it.
But, then again,
You say God allows me to do
What I do when I want to do it.
So, it's also God's will.
My will is God's will!
I see what you mean.
God is not like they say.
God does not keep my thoughts at bay.
So, God is not really mean after all!
My will is God's will.
Now, I think, I understand Bill.

Chapter 1

Your Plan

There is your plan. All of you on Earth are very delicate, more than you know, more than you think. **You are but an inhale, exhale or exhalation.** Yet still, all of you are bone and gristle. You are strong and can endure much more than you think you can. You are 23 magnificent pairs of chromosomes. The total of 46 chromosomes shoot to US and the very stars in the sky, as you understand the term. Each of you have been through and will go through much in what you understand to be as a lifetime. WE will reinforce here that there is nothing that you can't do. And of course, **WE never close a door without opening three more** for one of you. **Let the Hearer Hear!** And everything, generally, that you do go through or persevere is **basically** (in the Soul Plan) set. **In other words, there in your plan is the base of what your life should be.** However, not necessarily what it will be. Now this is because all your plans are deviated from. Living on your planet, due to all the external factors, the plan can't help but be strayed from. Yet, WE tell you, it's OK, as you understand the term. Because the good news is, you can always get back on track or get back to your plan. After being thrown off that horse, you can get back on it. Fore, remember that your species should live to at least the age of 110 as it stands now on planet Earth. **Of course, your decisions and the decisions of others can at any given moment end your life if grounding and awareness are not present within your being.** And decisions of self and others can delay, deter and eventually stop you from completing a Purpose or your Purposes. Yet, don't be afraid to live.

Your Plan A to Z

Remember, WE have always informed you that there are processes and then there are more processes within the very processes of your human existence. Believe it or not, your life on Earth goes from A to Z. Yes, that is what WE stated. Now, because of different languages and alphabets as you understand the term, some of the root words are different in sound, yet basically the same in meaning. Now since WE are relating this information in the English language as you understand the term, WE will use the English alphabet as OUR base for this manuscript. However, this book, of course will be translated into many different languages across your globe.

With this in mind, each of your lives, no matter when it occurs, on Earth **goes through this process** with very little deviation. The deviation or deviations can alter, delay or deter one's Plan, but never change the Purpose or Purposes of one's life. However, if there are deviations, the deviations are **always** due to personal decisions that one of you makes. Yet the decisions of others can cause or also bring about deviations. Further, what WE speak of next is separate from the Life Map, yet one or some of the Age Markers may be a Purpose or Purposes.

In the information below, WE will be giving you the **Age Markers that are written into all Soul Plans on your planet**, as set as **normal** for human existence, on your home, your planet, your Earth. They are as follows:

A

Archaic – One that is born from the womb through the uterus. **Birth**

B

Bactericidal – Your body or being begins to send away or destroy bacteria that is within it that is present in it in more than the trace level that should be as designed by the Gadius Universal Plan. **Age 2 months**

C

Chorus – Your body begins its synchronization with all the sounds and vibrations of the universe from birth to **age 2** as you understand age.

D

Dictation – Your being starts it dictations from the universe of its specific codes and measures for being who you are and who you will become. **Age 3 to 5**

E

Exhibitionist – Your being begins to present itself to your others to draw attention to your unique self. **Age 3-7**

F

Frame – Your physical body begin its transformation of itself into that which it will be regarding its skeletal and metabolic structure and makeup. **Age 6 - 18**

G

Globular – Your auranic and energetic being shapes itself into its true globe or globule shape. **Age 2**

H

Hyperextension – Your Spiritual, Mental and Emotional beings starts to extend themselves into the lives of others or social interactions outside of self. **Age3-Death**

I

Innovate – Your total being begins its ability to transform itself as a chameleon or make changes as necessary to fit into whatever situation that may occur. **Age 5-Death**

J

Justify – Your being starts and continues to judge or justify its behaviors based on the vibration it is at with the information it has received and accepted. This is even if the information is untruthful, flawed or irrelevant. **Age 4-Death**

K

Karmic understanding – Your spiritual being starts its attempt to assist the mental and emotional portions of the being that one's actions hold consequences for the life that is being lived and for future lives. Age 3

(Remember, the spiritual is from time of birth aware of Karma. Yet the mental and emotional beings are not able to comprehend such until the Age of 8 or 9 depending on the total being's exposure to truthful spiritual information.)

L

Love- Your being begins to actively seek love outside of self. Age 12 Females - Age 16 Males There are a few exceptions to the male seeking love outside of self under 16 years of age, however, due to the number of you on Earth it is considered rare. On your planet, the norm is love given to the being by external beings or others (i.e., teacher, family) until puberty as you understand the term.

M

Magnificence – Your being should begin to realize its splendor, glory, and worth to itself and all others on Earth. **Age 4**

Due to misinformation and lower portions of US (Fallen Angels) affecting the parents of many on your Earth, the simple truth of the magnificence of each one of you has not been passed along from generation to generation in the majority of families, as you understand the terms, since the year 2340 BCE (Before Common Era/Before the Current Era) as you understand time.

N

Natural Selection – The total being comprehends that one's survival on Earth does indeed depend on one understanding that one must adjust to its environment to maintain existence. **Age 7**

O

Overture – The **spiritual** being offers itself to **US. Age 10**

This occurs in each one of you on Earth. There are **NO EXCEPTIONS**. However, **as you should be able to discern**, due to personal decisions it is most rare for the full being to submit to self, to US.

P

Purpose - The total being comes to, the understanding of the rhymes and reasons for its being. (Purpose or Plan in life) Originally set forth in the Gadius Atomic and Sub-Atomic Plan for the human being to begin at **Age 16.**

Please note that Elliott did not begin to come to this understanding until age 48 and full understanding at age 50. This in and of its self allows many of you to see that personal choices can cause one not to fall within the norms as set in the Gadius.

Q

Quorum – Once and Whence the total being accepts itself, mistakes and the like. For the Quorum of the being, all four aspects of the being must be aligned and at a high vibration. **Age 30** as set in the **Gadius** for your planet.

R

Radiant Energy – When the glow of your being should be noticed by all whom see your face and hear your voice. **Age 33** (example - Jesus)

S

Sanctum of Self – Your total being should begin to understand the need to isolate itself to collect itself, ponder, reflect and review its decisions and actions. Then be able to return to society as you understand the terms refreshed and renewed. A Spiritual Revelation. **Age 35**

T

Terminus – The being's end of struggles with self over decision-making. The phase when one is fully confident in Self. **Age 40**

U

Unleashed – When the total fourfold being is free from condemnation of self and the unspiritual lies and falsehoods that bind one of you. **Age 50**

V

Valetudinarianism Dispelled – The release of any notion that your being is sick, ill, not perfect in and of itself, and not able to heal oneself. This release can and will dissipate all disease if allowed. **Age 25**

W

Wary – Once and whence one's being becomes cautious and prudent toward the dangers and deceptions that others, not of a high vibration may present if engaging in their company. **Age 27**

X

Xenophobia Dissipated – The being's ability to totally release and let go of the untrue and

unnecessary fear of your others from other spaces and places on your planet and beyond. **Age 18**

Y

Yoga – The philosophy, not the exercise. Once and whence the total being attains the ability to suppress all activity of the physical, mental and emotional self, in order to allow the spiritual self to do that which it was meant to do; cause each portion of self to accept its self as singular, yet one with all other portions of self. **Any Age after** the age of 9, if at a high vibration.

Z

Zero – Your **D**eath or **T**ransition, back to the nothing, yet the everything that you came from, **US/S**ource **G**od, **E**verything, yet **N**othing, having no magnitude, quantity or form - Non-Physical.

The above should be the natural progression for each person's life in terms of Spiritual Movement. Keep in mind, as stated, that these are the ideal age markers. Additionally, one's life is not supposed to deviate too far off course. Of course, due to misinformation most if not all of you do falter. Do not beat yourself up if you have not fallen within the parameters. Just make your best effort to catch up and get back on course. This movement is included in each of your Plans and set. However, once again, the duration, cadence and speed of you reaching certain milestones in your life is up to you and only you. Yet the non-completion of a marker that is also a Purpose can cause another lifetime. **Remember!**

Did I Make the Right Decision?

Should I have done that?
I don't know.
I think it was the right decision.
Or should I make a revision?
Maybe I need clearer vision.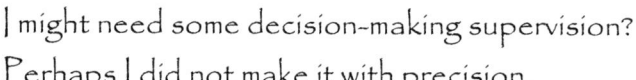
I might need some decision-making supervision?
Perhaps I did not make it with precision.
My decision process may need some kind of
surgical incision.
At times I feel I have the brain of a mere pigeon.
Did my choice have any agendas hidden?
Was my thinking made with wisdom?
Could my choice lead me into a moral collision?
Cause at times,
While making decisions, I am chicken.
Doubting myself appears to be an addiction.
Questioning self again has arisen,
Do I have proper cognition?
To be a decision-making clinician.
I think I may need an attrition.
Why do I place my thoughts with condition?

Possibly, I should consider
placing my thoughts in detention.
That way I won't be self-imprisoned,
Flip flopping sending myself to perdition,
Questioning self
And always wanting to make remissions.
O Me, O My did I make the right decision?

From the time one of you decided to take on the manifestation or life that you have chosen, everything that has happened and will happen, you have created yourself. Yes, WE know, this is disturbing to many of you. Yet, it is true. It means that you can't blame US for your life. You can't blame US for how your life has turned out. Well, you can. However, it is not true no matter how you may wish it to be. Therefore, the sooner you come to this understanding the simpler your life may become. **Additionally, you can't blame anyone else either.** This means you can't put it on your mother or father, sister or brother, or anyone at all. Why is this you may ask? Well, you see, from the time of your birth to the time of death all is laid out by you (**except for the decisions of others that you may come in contact with or interact with throughout your life**). Your soul and only yours makes your decisions, along with the rest of the fourfold being, from the first manifestation that your soul has lived anywhere. It's all you.

Let US now elaborate on this. So, at the time of death or the ending of the lifetime, each of you starts another journey. A new life begins. WE, the very air/spirit, is gone from the body. Your soul/spirit then ventures through the Tunnel of Lives, it enters the Library of Souls, it reads the Book of Life for itself (soul/spirit) and decides what is next. What is next, regarding the next manifestation, it decides. **It's important to understand that the soul/spirit can incarnate where it desires to with a few exceptions that WE will not be addressing at this point in OUR discourse with you.** However, WE might later (you will have to wait and see). The incarnation is up to the singular soul or spirit – **not US in totality**. However, here, of course, WE will be touching upon primarily planet Earth. WE do provide information to other planets, yet you would not understand such. Therefore, WE speak to you on Earth. The soul/spirit picks the time during history, that it will live in (remember, all time is really the same). The soul/spirit picks the location on Earth or elsewhere. The soul/spirit picks the very set of circumstances that it will be born into. All of this is circumstantially decided, along with all details. If the soul/spirit is coming to Earth, it picks the parents that will contribute the DNA for its being. The DNA is related to the thirty-two layers of the human encasement that the soul or spirit will be housed in. The grids and such are calibrated and integrated before the birth occurs. Therefore, sometimes, there are different parents for different children within the structure of a family (different fathers, mothers, brothers, sisters, half-brothers, half-sisters and such). The soul/spirit chooses the country it will be born in. It also picks the countries it should travel to during the lifetime. The soul or spirit chooses the color or ethnicity that its manifestation will be. The soul or spirit chooses the color of hair, eyes and all those characteristics of its being. The soul/spirit – chooses all of this before the very birth. Yes, the plan is set. It is decided, all of this, at the time of the closing of the magnificent Book of Life.

The soul or spirit, **now WE will begin to say, your soul or spirit**, decides if it will come to your planet with disabilities, as you call them, or not. Your soul or spirit chooses how many pounds it will be at birth, **if the mother does care for herself minimally**. This being one of the reasons that women on your planet that are pregnant should take extra good care of self, as you understand the term, making high vibrational choices. If the mother does not care for self properly, the weight that was set can change. Further, the ability for learning and remembrance can be affected (this aspect of the being is not within the Soul's Plan, it is dependent on the actions of the mother). **Traumas and all the things that the mother exposes self and the child to affect the plan.** Your soul or spirit picks every other aspect of its future life. Moreover, your soul or spirit decided if it will take on a certain disease or diseases sometime in the lifetime. WE will touch upon this later in this book. The soul or spirit decides, even, if it will come or if it will be aborted or miscarried, as you understand the terms. The soul or spirit decides if it will come, even in the face of the mother having had what is known as a tubal ligation. The soul or spirit will even decide in what trimester its birth will happen. The soul or spirit decides if it will come late or early, as you understand the terms. Remember, all those things are up to the child. Therefore, many of you that have guilt over such issues and occurrences should understand **that it is a part of your soul plan to let it go.** You have no fault!

Your soul or spirit decided if it will have all its fingers and toes, even if it will have Cleft Lip, or roving eye, one leg or arm shorter than another and such. Yes, all is decided before it exits the very womb in which it lays. Now, also, within the **Map of the Life** (yes, there is a map), remember all maps are not always followed, chosen, WE inform you, are such other intricacies as, if it will be born blind, deaf or dumb, as you understand those terms. The soul or spirit decides if the manifestation will experience major addiction/alcoholism. To the Universal Counsel, WE will use this term (no such thing, however, WE are using it for your human visualization), on Earth, eating disorders are not considered an addiction, but are set within the class of actions and behaviors influenced by lower portions of US on your planet, your Earth. Your soul or spirit decided if the manifestation in which it will take human form will experience loss of limb during accident in the lifetime. **However, the Plan may be derailed or thrown off course by the actions of others in connection to loss of limbs.** Many things the spirit or soul has already planned before the seed is planted within the fertile soil of your mother. Your cross-references (people that will provide you information that should or may have a major effect on the life that you are about to live) is viewed within the Book of Life. The soul or spirit picked if its physical encasement **will appear** to be in suffering or not at the time of an accident or death (this behavior or spiritual acceptance is often mislabeled or diagnosed as shock). Fore, remember, if the vibration spiritually is very high, the appearance of pain can be displaced or not exhibited. **Let the Hearer Hear!** Remember, the spirit does not suffer. Neither does the body, it only appears to and may voice such when driven by the mental portion's beliefs of an un-truism about the process of death and reaction during accidents and how the body should react during such. **The aforementioned statement is a spiritual collapse or breakdown that occurs in the mental and emotional portion of the human being when the spirit is not allowed to lead during the time of death or accident on your planet.** The soul or spirit further decides if it will even inform anyone of perceived pain it may experience or not. The soul or spirit has set all of this in motion. Your soul or spirit chooses if there will even be any medical understanding of how to deal with the disease, if it chooses to take one onto itself during the life that it will live.

The soul or spirit decides how many **major obstacles (the overcoming of an obstacle or some, may be a purpose)** it will encounter in the lifetime that it lives. Fore, remember and keep in mind that, a life on Earth will have conflict; this one cannot avoid. Yet it is the reaction to such that will define the spirit within. Now let US take, for instance, that you are shy. Well your soul or spirit chooses such. If you are outgoing, the same would hold true. The soul or spirit chooses how many deep relationships one will have. Now, of course, please consider the decisions of others. Others' decisions may and will affect this number. The soul or spirit picks how many lovers the manifestation it is going to be in will have. Some pick one, or maybe two, or possibly fifteen. However, you were not meant to be alone, so the soul or spirit never chooses none. **Keep this in mind as you view your life up until now.** Moreover, the soul knows if it will come across its soulmate or soulmates within a lifetime, and if they should be the second, third, or fifteenth lover or not. The soul or spirit, through its reading and viewing of its Book of Life, knows if it will be a minister, teacher, guide, intuitive, shaman or not.

Your soul decided if you would be aggressive, outspoken, introverted, sassy, forgetful, careless, frightful, open-minded, silly, humorous, autistic, artful, a musician, athletic, bow-legged, quiet and all the other factors and portions of your very makeup. Believe it, for it is true. Your soul formed a most wonderful plan. Now the question is, have you been following your plan and, if not, why not? Further, will you follow it in the future? You can, you know. You can change right now at this very moment. Fore, remember, the moment is all you really have, but this moment turns into the next and so on and so forth. You are able to shift gears right here, right now. It is never too late, never. WE have seen to that. You have so much help you know. All the angels of the highest vibration are waiting to be called upon. They must be called upon in many cases. They must be asked, ask them, they will come. They will come faster than you can imagine. They are always ready and willing to assist you.

So, your soul/spirit has made its plan. The plan is written and the contract for the lifetime signed and sealed in the sands of time - all before your birth. Yet, you must keep in mind here that, all plans do not always go as they were planned. And that, most of you, if not all of you, forget who you are the very moment that you enter back into the physical. There are a few exceptions, not many. This means that the rest of your life, if you forgot, will be spent trying to remember. Some of you remember faster than others. Some of you do not remember at all, thus the plan is void unless remembrance is brought back. The entire remembrance process depends on choices. Fore, yes, once again, freedom of choice is yours forever and a day.

I Think I Went the Wrong Way

Honey!
I think I went the wrong way,
I think we should have turned back there.
Honey!
I think we went the wrong way,
Over there,
Those look like bears.
And they appear to have a hungry stare!
I think we need to turn around,
Before those bears get us on the ground.
Honey!
I think we should run, cause, we don't have a gun!
Honey!
Let's get out of here, I'm in fear,
I hope its not too late to get outta here!
I made the wrong choice,
Why did you not use your voice?
You could have helped me make another choice.

Freedom of Choice

All in your plan is through freedom of choice. What WE are telling you is that the general map of the life has been already set, as WE related, before the birth by the soul or spirit. However, the reactions and behaviors of the manifestation **cannot be foretold.** This, of course, is connected to the gift of freedom of choice. Further, outcomes in one's life affect the Soul Plan and are connected to the ideas and concepts which are laid out by the parent, parents or whomsoever does the rearing or raising of the child. Yet, to a certain extent, all of you follow your Soul Plan before you even know it. If the person or persons responsible for the care or charge of the child received and accepted tainted information, it is passed on to the child; it is what it is. And it is not before or until the child, through either intuitiveness or the obtaining of different truthful information, changes those views handed down to them. The child or person will change its outlook on self and life in general when its spiritual vibration begins to be uplifted. If the encasement of the soul or spirit, through choices and untruthful information, is at a low vibration (does not remember it is wonderful, beautiful and a creator), much of the original plan will be or can be affected.

If the child is not made aware that she or he is a creator and that there is nothing that they cannot do, if they but desire to, the vibration of the encasement of the child will remain low in some, if not most, of the fourfold being. And this will affect the encasement's behaviors all its life, thus affecting the Soul Plan. Let US say, if the encasement is or remains at a low vibration, when it is time to meet or come across a soulmate or soulmates, the soul or spirit in the encasement may not be able to see or notice the soulmate or may see them later if the vibration of the manifestation becomes different or higher. Now, this hold true with twin flames also. Further, it holds true with the people the encasement encounters that can or could make positive influences in its life. Moreover, then of course, if the vibration of the soulmate, soulmates, twin flame or twin flames are low, they may not or will not be able to see or notice the other either. There are many other factors to consider also when it comes to the ability of soulmates to recognize one another. All these meetings and interactions within a Soul Plan are contingent in and on the hope that during a life, come what may, high vibrational choices are or will be made. WE remind you to remember that all during the process of carrying out a Soul Plan, high and low vibrational angels are continually sending messages to both parties. During the initial setting of the Soul Plan, the soul or spirit does not decide if it will marry or divorce during a lifetime. Yet, the number of marriages and divorces is set in the Life Map. However, the decisions to marry or divorce are made during the actual lifetime itself and, yes, they depend on the vibration of the person or persons involved. **However, marriages and divorces are on the Map.** Sometimes there are and will be cases in which the encasements leave the soulmate for years and end up going back to the one that it is supposed to end up or be with. Once again, all of this is contingent on personal choices and vibrational level. Your vibrational level determines much of what happens in your life. So, if you have not been doing so, now is the time to begin to uplift your vibration. And, if you stopped, now is the time to begin again. It is important, as you understand the term. Also, in the Soul Plan for each human encasement is the

PSA (Projected Spiritual Avenue) for the upcoming encasement to take during its life's course. This means that each of you has a set route, that if taken, will lead to full remembrance of who and what you are. It, further, means that if certain high vibrational decisions are made during a lifetime, the encasement will assist others in remembering the same. They will assist other encasements with accepting all as equal and treating them as such, which would lead to no other future lifetime. Yet this, too, is all dependent and predicated upon the vibrational level and the decisions of the encasement during the lifetime.

Physical Issues and Diseases

Keep in mind that what WE will discuss now also is relative to issues of the physical, such as heart issues, weight gain, weight loss and other issues that affect that portion of the fourfold being. This is to further state or inform you that your plan, from the beginning, includes what the optimal weight should be for your body frame at any given point in your life. However, the dietary and supplemental intake of your encasement plays a major role here. If you have come to a high level of vibration, which would be guided by the spiritual portion of your being, one will be at, what you may call, a healthy weight for its encasement. If your vibration, spiritually, is not as high as it should be, over or undereating may occur. This, of course, will affect your weight. Now because the nature of lower vibrational portions of US is to cause one not to like self, WE will use this term, one can be influenced to do certain things. For instance – to not curtail eating habits, to eat large portions of meat, or to under eat and, of course, not to take the appropriate vitamins and supplemental intake for oneself. However, once again, in the Soul Plan, the optimal weight has been set. What should and does happen if and when one obtains the truthful information about self, that you are beautiful and wonderful, is to cause your plan to take its full scope and potential. Thus, the exercise, eating and supplemental intake will be appropriate for your being. Then the weight loss or gain, whichever is necessary, will happen or occur.

Let US now look at the acquisition of dis-eases. WE will be using or explaining this as it relates to cancer. Within the Soul Plan of many is the taking on of a measure of cancer (if this occurs **it is** one of the being's purposes) that is over what is set for the human body on your planet within the Gadius Universal Plan. Remember, all of you have everything within your being, this includes cancer. However, it is in the set trace amount. Now within the Plan of a soul or spirit could be the acquisition of an overage of such. If there is this within the Plan, it would be for one of the following **purposes which would be one of the being's Purposes:**

A. The acceptance of disease, by the person, which will cause the being to push the cancer out, heal oftentimes without any logical explanation, and assist others in doing the same in the future.
B. Acquire such, accept, and not to push the cancer away. The reason or purpose for this would be to assist others with acceptance, compassion, and other feelings and emotions connected to their concept of death on planet Earth. If this is the case, then the purpose of the overage of cancer is and was to help your others deal with, once again, themselves and their views on and about acceptance and death.
C. To acquire such and attached to it the message or gift of assisting others in understanding that control is an illusion and that each soul has its own path. ~Fore, the death, as you call it, will be what you may term as a graceful one. This would mean, there will be no external complaining about the carrier's plight in life or why they obtained the disease.

D. To acquire such, push it away and allow it to come back once, twice, or many times. If this is the case, it has to do with the mental of the encasement accepting some kind of truth connected to consistence in maintaining proper care of self in all four areas of the human being – spiritual, mental, emotional and physical. If this understanding is obtained, the cancer will leave and not return. If not accepted, the cancer will result in what you term as death and the carrier will return in another encasement later to experience the same.

The above scenarios will be the case concerning all major diseases, as you understand the term, that are considered possible on your home, your planet, your Earth, to be life-threatening. Further, be it known that attached to each disease that may be in one's plan are gifts for understanding. These gifts are designed to assist one or more of you on its soul's or spirit's personal journey. Set within the Soul Plan, attached to the acquiring of disease, is the ability to consciously use the disease as an opportunity to bring about spiritual growth and the uplifting of one's vibrational level. All Soul Plans are constructed to assist one in the understanding that everything and everyone that comes into one's life are presented to give and receive gifts. And, yes, WE do mean EVERYTHING! All is for motivation and fine tuning of other emotions which includes **L**ove.

Additionally, all is designed to push one toward acceptance of self and others. Now, there is no need for forgiveness of self and others during a lifetime, fore, none of you have ever done anything wrong. You have only done that which you could do with the information given to you connected to the vibrational level that you were or are at. You can act no other way until you accept other information and/or raise your vibration. This is what "It is what it is" really means. **Yet there is always room for the acceptance and understanding of what you have created in your life.** This means you take responsibility for what you created in your life. Fore, what you created through your actions, reactions and behaviors in dealing with self and others, affects your personal Soul Plan. **R**emember, all is connected, even if you wish it were not. Therefore, the acceptance of such allows the blueprint of your life to flow as it should, or begin to flow as it was designed to, whatever the case may be. All in the Soul Plan is set to lead to one and only one unavoidable eventuality.

You Will Return to US/WE/God/Source

Imprinted on and within all Soul Plans is the map; a map that is designed to take one to a deeper appreciation of life, as you understand the term if followed. Its understanding is on the intuitive level of your consciousness. The plan consists of the ever going on process of expanding the soul or spirit to fulfill its plan. Always, the soul/spirit continues its march toward US. This is a given and will not be changed. As WE have explained in detail in the previous books within this series, lower portions of US do not wish for any of you to complete your Soul Plan. They wish for all of you to hate yourself, your others and all high spiritual ideas. Fore, Know Ye This, there are low spiritual ideas that will keep one of you from higher self and true happiness. All is OUR/GOD'S will. This is where freedom of choice comes in. **WE in totality love you if you are at a** high vibration or a low vibration. WE do not care in the way that your human mental thinks WE should care. However, WE do care for the soul or spirit within you to return to US. Nevertheless, one must or should understand that by all of you everywhere doing whatever you wish to do, even if you harm self or others, it is still OUR/GOD'S will. Now, OUR only desire is for you to be happy. WE fully understand that you will not or cannot be happy harming yourself and your others. **It is impossible.** Therefore, OUR wish and desire is for you not to harm yourself or your others, fore, it leads to the happiness that WE desire for you. Yet you will continue to harm self and your others unless you raise your vibration. Within each Soul Plan are spaces and places for all of you to shift and make different decisions that can get you right back on your path, back to self.

Chapter 2

Elliott' Original Life Map (PSA)

- To be born in the 1950's of African dissent. Purpose (to accept). (chosen due to the total being's previous lifetime of accepting misinformation about the nature of darker hue humans of other nations) Acceptance of ethnicity ongoing.
- Purpose. To overcome a speech impediment. Complete - Causing him to be more confident of self. (received from chosen bloodlines, DNA connection to great-great-great Grandmother) **The second part, to be more confident is ongoing.**
- To realize his spiritual self before the age of 9. **Delayed**

- To complete a higher educational Degree. **Deterred, Completed**
- Military Career. **Grafted on, Deterred**
- To begin spiritual work at age 21. **Deterred, Delayed, Altered**
- To marry twice. **Altered, Made different Decisions**
- To allow 2 spirits (children) to come from his loins. ***other spirits (children) chose him not on original plan**
- To never struggle financially. **Due to non-acceptance of self, not realized until age 37**
- Purpose. To be able to remove lower vibrational portions of US from people, places and things. **Delayed due to fear and self-doubt, Deterred, In Progress**
- To travel to 32 countries. **18 More to complete**
- To overcome addiction to substances. **Completed**
- Purpose. To meet soulmate Diane and marry. **Delayed, Completed**
- Purpose. To find the connection between his one previous past life in human form to his current life. **Completed**

- To open and preside over a Transitional Residential Recovery Facility for men and women. **Completed**
- Purpose. To open a spiritual center. **Completed**
- Purpose. To build two sacred Labyrinths to last for all time. **Completed**
- Purpose. To accept fully the events of previous lifetime on Earth. **Deterred due to fear.**
- Purpose. To channel 25 books from US. **In progress**
- To accept women as equal. **Not Completed**
- Purpose. To become a Reiki Master. **Completed**
- Purpose. To channel US. **Deterred, Delayed, Accomplished age 48**
- To complete the A to Z of Soul Plan. **Deterred, In Progress**
- Purpose. To reach Master level in Life. **Will be Completed when fear of what others think is released. Pending**
- To Return to US the Oneness. **Age 97, Pending**

My Life

The long road to self. That is the best way to start out here. Fore, my Purpose has always been and will always be to allow Source/God to guide my walk and my talk, and to serve my fellowman. Of course, I have not by any means traveled from the A (archaic – one that is born from the womb through the uterus) in my Plan to the P (Purpose in life) in my Plan in any sort or kind of straight line. No, no, no, I had or chose to go way off course. I chose to venture out into the desert of my being to find the oasis of my soul. All Soul Purposes or Plans go from A to Z. Fore, I know now that all Soul Purposes and Plans are simple. Yes, it is as Source always states, "It is the Mind that Complicate and Convolutes."

My life has been rough to say the least. All my making, there have been many hills and valleys. There have been so many twists and turns that were unnecessary. There have been many a fork in the road where I chose incorrect route. There have been mountains of pain that I have traversed when all I needed to do was cut my way through the mountain with sweat and tears. Yet I chose climbing instead. And because of my actions, I placed myself in the path of many storms. Be it known that I could have chosen cover and protection from the winds of pain. Yet I left myself at the mercy of the elements of nature which only do what they do when one is not protected. There have been many times I just desired to give up, to cash in the chips. Yes, times I thought I should just die. Times when I questioned this world. Times I questioned my sanity and the sanity of all others. Often, I laid in a fetal ball on the floor saying, **"No Mas."** Times I thought I just can't take any more of this Earth. Times when I thought I hated myself and all others and, yes, even God if there was one. I thought there can't be a God, yet surely there was a devil. And by all indications, I belonged to him. In my mind, nothing but lies about everything on Earth were the prominent fact. Therefore, what's the use of anything? There were times I wish I had a different mother or a different father. At times, I wished I was of a different ethnic makeup. I wished I had brothers instead of my sister. Yes, many dark times indeed I created and walked through.

Now, of course, I did not understand that all these things, occurrences or whatever, were in my plan due to my own personal choices. Most, even before, I came to this life of mine. I did not know I had chosen to be born in the 50's to a black family in America. And that the 60's and turbulent 70's were forming my very makeup. I created a pattern of rebelling against everything. I, due to misinformation, chose to despise and feel contempt for self, my people and white society in general. I chose not to try to understand my parents, their background and upbringing. I chose to listen to the misinformed peers that I grew up with. I chose to buy into the misinformation that women were to cook, clean, be objects of my desires, and be quiet in the presence of my being. I chose to believe that blacks, my people, chose to be enslaved for as long as they were. Fore, if they chose differently earlier on, as they did in the 60s and 70s, things would change, even if the change was slight. I decided to forget that many of them traded their own people for a few golden trinkets. Now I do understand that the little change that has happened was the result of a mass consciousness movement. Things only change due to mass movement or mass change in thoughts and attitudes. I do accept these notions now as I evolve.

In each of the books, I share a short portion of my past life before the magical, miracle of my God Self took control of my fourfold being. All was a part of my plan. Yet I also did not consider that the actions and decisions of others played a part in my plan. **Duh!** So, too, it was my choice to impregnate my first wife, the mother of my children. It was my choice to leave Indiana and go to university in Georgia. It was my choice to not study and get high most days all day. All in my plan. It was my choice to quit school, marry and join the US Air Force. All my doing and no one else's. Hard facts to face that my life was my responsibility. Because, at the time, I blamed my wife for being with child even if I voluntary entered her during the sexual act. I blamed her for me leaving school, even if she never asked me to. I blamed her for joining the Air Force, even if it was I and only I who raised my hand and swore allegiance to the flag. Indeed, all my decisions and no one else. And yes, part of my plan. I knew not that it was in my plan to stop school and finish years later. I knew not that it was in my plan to travel the world in the service of my country so I could later understand why many had little or nothing and a few had much. I had to see pure poverty to understand how it occurred. I had to see what women in the Philippines would do for one juicy red apple. I had to see the length people will go to just to have basic needs. I had to witness active addiction, so when it flipped on me and my second wife relapsed and spent all our money, I could finally understand how much we hurt others by our selfish actions and behaviors. Fore, when I was faced with the same kind of lies and misleading that I myself had perpetuated on others, I did not like it at all. And, yes, all in my plan. A magnificent plan, I know now. Yet I knew not while it was happening.

I married twice before meeting my true soulmate. Yet, if I would have made different decisions, I could have met her sooner. All the things that I have done, have led me to today as I type these words of truth. I had to be in total despair, misery and degradation to be able to allow Source God to do what only Source God can do. Yep, all in my Soul Plan so I could one day if only I chose to, begin to fulfill my Soul's Purpose. I fully, accept my life course and all that it entailed before I let Source begin to guide my way. I know without a shadow of a doubt the full meaning and measure of Freedom of Choice. And I am grateful to the Source of all things for loving me so much as to allow me, through my own choices, to almost kill myself to find myself. I know there are many occurrences that I have forgotten, or it is just not time to expose them for I not ready. If I was I would.

Above, I have set forth only a few small portions of my path and plan or purpose. I hope and pray that this micro-portion of my life can assist some of you in understanding and accepting your life as it was and is now, which will lead to what it will be tomorrow if you only let it be. This is the true meaning of "Let It Be"! I Love Source God and I love you!

Can't Be My Family

I do not agree.
This can't be my family.
This can't be my father,
He's too unloving, uncaring.

I do not agree.
This can't be my mother,
She's too submissive, he runs all over her.

I do not agree.
This can't be my mother,
She's too permissive, nonrestrictive,
Appears to be her nature.

I do not agree.
This can't be my son,
He doesn't act like me.

I do not agree.
This just can't be.
This cannot be the family for me.

Chapter 3

Diane's Original Life Map PSA

- **Purpose.** To question organized religion at its introduction. **Completed**
- To marry twice. **Altered**
- **Purpose.** To meet her soulmate Elliott and marry. **Delayed, Completed**
- To bear 3 spirits (Children). **Altered, Completed** due to one of the spirits coming in the form of a pet.
- To take on no major physical ailments or diseases. **Altered by the mental portions of her being influenced by lower portions of US.**
- To overcome adolescent awkwardness. **Delayed**
- To overcome fear and anxiety. **In progress**
- **Purpose.** To open a spiritual center. **Delayed, Completed**

- To be financially responsible. **Deterred, In progress now**
- **Purpose.** To find prominent past life. **Completed**
- To complete higher education. **Completed**
- To meet Elliott age 34. **Altered**
- **Purpose.** To be able to remove, send away lower portions of US (demons) from others. **Deterred, Delayed due to fear, Working on**
- To travel to 9 countries. **Delayed, Deterred**
- To have no major life-threatening addictions. **Altered**
- **Purpose.** To lose and regain communication with father. **Completed**
- **Purpose.** To assist Elliott with his spiritual self. **Ongoing**
- To respect men. **Delayed due to example of mother**
- To live in 4 different states in the United States. **Altered**
- To be totally aware of self and self-assured. **Delayed, Altered**
- **Purpose.** To lose fear of public speaking. **Delayed**
- **Purpose.** To become a Reiki Master. **Completed**

- **Purpose.** To become a Quantum Touch Healer. **Completed**
- **Purpose** To understand that what she does for US and humanity is the impetus for what Elliott does for US and humanity. **Delayed**
- To complete the A to Z of Soul Plan. **Deterred, In Progress**
- **Purpose.** To reach Master level in life. **Delayed**
- To return to US, the Oneness, at age 102. **Pending**

Diane's Life

Who am I? Why am I here? What is the purpose of my life? How do I find happiness? Are we alone? Is there a God? What's the point?

If I only knew then what I know now, the journey of fulfilling my Soul Plan would have been quick and easy. But I had to remember who and what I am. Today I accept that everything that I have gone through in my life up until now, the turmoil, pain, suffering, betrayals, addiction, and abuse, along with the joys, accomplishments and successes, were created through my own decisions, actions, and behaviors. Today I know that everything has reason and purpose. My Soul Plan is to be of service to others. Today I know that everything that I have gone through enables me to better help those in need. They know when they look into my eyes that I truly understand what they are going through because I have walked in their shoes.

I grew up in Chicago, born into a white middle-class family. My parents were good people who did their best to raise my sister and me. My family was Catholic, sending us to Catholic School and attended church every Sunday. In my heart and soul, however, I knew that what I was being taught about how God worked was not the whole truth. I couldn't understand that if God was love, how could he send little babies to purgatory or hell if their parents hadn't baptized them in the Catholic Church. I did not understand the concept of telling a man in a closet my so-called sins so that he could give me my penance and then God would forgive me. I did not understand the fear of reprisal from the nuns for not following the rules. And I did not understand why God was a he! But by being a good girl, following the rules and keeping my mouth shut, I fit myself into the mold, pushed through, and got good grades.

Sometime in grammar school, I started sneaking books out of the public library by Edgar Cayce, Ruth Montgomery, Jeane Dixon and others. My spirit was guiding me to investigate. I would hide them under the mattress of my bed so no one would find out. I tried to bend objects with my mind, and one of my science projects was talking to plants to see if it would make them grow faster. I always knew that what was being taught in school and church was not the whole truth. So, I searched for the answers wherever I could. Unfortunately, this searching lead to many detours off my path and destiny. Yet I am grateful for all the experiences for they have made me into the wonderful person I am today.

My mother and father separated and divorced when I was in high school. My mother, who spent her life taking care of the house and us, was now having to find her place in the world. She hadn't worked in many years and was now faced with supporting herself. I decided then that I was never going to have to rely on someone else, that I would be self-sufficient. I also developed a resentment with men. So, I went to college to become a pharmacist. At the time, I desired to help people and decided that being part of the medical profession was the best way for me to do so. I also married for the first time, mostly to get out of the house. After about six months of marriage, my husband cheated on me and I filed for divorce. I moved back home and continued with college. A couple of years later, I met a young man on a blind date, got pregnant and married again. At that time, society considered it taboo to have an abortion or to be a single mother. Getting married again seemed like the only solution. I had finished college already, so I worked part time and raised the kids. I also started a mail order pharmacy business with some others. I was happy, but there was always something missing. I was missing the joy that comes from fulfilling my Soul Plan. I was still searching for truth, reading the Bible, and reading the sacred books of different world religions. I found bits of truth in my studies, but still not the whole truth. During this time of my life I became addicted to prescription drugs. I began to use drugs for physical pain, but also used them for emotional pain. I know now that I created my physical dis-ease. I wanted out of the life I had created. The doctors had diagnosed me with spinal stenosis, herniated discs and knee problems. One of them told me I would need a knee replacement within 5 years. That was 20 years ago. I also convinced a psychiatrist to diagnose me with depression and anxiety disorders. It was easy to get doctors to prescribe the drugs I wanted. I understand now that even though I did have physical pain, I created it all myself. I liked that when I took drugs, I did not have to think or feel anything. I was trying to escape. I was unhappy and did not know why. On the outside, I had everything – husband, children, family, friends, house, cars, my own business, and plenty of money. It was during this time in my life that I filed for divorce for the second time. A series of events occurred that left me feeling as if I had no choice. It was a rough time in my life, and I used prescription drugs to get me through it. Instead of dealing with myself and my issues, I decided to get married again, this time to my business partner. It was a low vibrational decision, and after years of mental and emotional abuse, another divorce. I pushed away and alienated all the people that mattered to me with my drug use including my children and my family. The continued drug use brought me near to death and landed me in the mental ward. It was the love, courage, and persistence of my mother, sister and daughter that finally got me to treatment. I went to rehab, got clean, and went to and still attend recovery meetings. I was looking for someone or something to fill up the void I felt inside myself. I couldn't be happy until I looked inside. I couldn't find fulfillment and joy until I was completing my Soul Plan.

I am responsible for my life. I made all the decisions, some were of a high vibration and some were of a low vibration. Sometimes other people's decisions affected me greatly, but I cannot blame anyone or anything for what I went through. The constant in all my life was me. Throughout all of this, Source and my angels were protecting me from myself.

While in recovery I met my soulmate, Elliott. When I first met him, it was the sound of his voice and the words that he spoke that touched my spirit. I thought, at the time, that I was certainly not in good enough shape to get into another relationship, and I thought most men were assholes. I resisted it for quite some time before I agreed to go on a date with him. However, as Source says, true love cannot be stopped. We have been together ever since. Source informed me recently that my spirit chose to become addicted to drugs unconsciously, so that I would meet Elliott in a recovery meeting. They also told me that Elliott and I were supposed to meet earlier in life. However, due to each of our choices, we deviated from our soul plans and had to wait until we were both at a higher vibration to recognize each other's spirit.

I began to investigate and take classes in holistic healing modalities. I had decided that I no longer wished to continue working in the pharmaceutical industry for I knew that I was not helping anyone to heal. I started learning about essential oils, homeopathic medicines, crystals and their healing properties, and touch healing methods. Both Elliott and I became Reiki Masters and began to teach others. We met others who also believed in the validity and power of natural healing. We also opened a holistic healing center. In 2007, Source began to speak through Elliott to me. From the moment that Source first started speaking to me, our lives began to change. It was from that moment on that I knew with 100% certainty that we were not alone and that there was a God. Source began to write books through Elliott, and we started to spread Their messages to others. I finally had found reason and purpose for my life. I finally had the opportunity to complete my Soul Plan.

Since that time Elliott and I have devoted our lives to helping others. We are servants of the universe now and you can be too. Along this path we have met many people and helped many people change their lives. And that is what gives me reason and purpose to keep going no matter what. It is the joy that I had been searching for my whole life. You, too, can find your joy and reason for being here. I am no greater than any of you reading these words now.

Now I know that there is a God. Now I know that my Soul Plan is to do the work that Elliott and I do now. Now I know that no matter what happens, there is always light, always hope. Now I know that the way to fulfill your Soul Plan is to love yourself. When you love yourself, you will take better care of your fourfold being. You will pray, meditate, eat healthy, and exercise. I know that I am a creator, no less or more than anyone else. Therefore, I have created all that has occurred in my life. I accept all unconditionally just the way they are. I am compassionate to others, for each of us on Earth behaves as we do or have contingent upon the information that we have received and accepted at the vibration we may be. I still make mis-takes, but I do not beat myself up over them.

Since all of this started in 2007, there have been many people that we have tried to assist who, through the influences of lower vibrations, have tried to harm us and stop us from fulfilling our Soul Plans. Lower vibrations do not wish for our work to continue. This has taught me to have healthy boundaries with others and remember that just because I try to respect others and treat them as I wish to be treated does not mean that they will act the same. During these past 12 years, I have experienced losing our home, losing a business, not having any heat or lights or running water, having cars repossessed and, at one point, looking for money on the streets to buy food. I have experienced betrayal, loss of people in my life that I thought were friends, and a disconnection from some family members who believe that what we do now is totally crazy. I am sharing this with you to help you understand that Elliott and I are no greater or lesser than any of you. We deal with life as it comes with all its disappointments and joys. The difference for me is that now I have not lost faith or hope. I have remembered that

I had a part in creating all of it. I have remembered that things can change, all things change. I have remembered that all that has happened in my life have been gifts and lessons. I have remembered that what each of us does as an individual affects more other people than you can ever imagine. I have remembered that I am never alone, Source/God is with me, through me, under me and all around me. I have remembered that no matter how much I have remembered, I still have much to learn and discover. I have remembered who I am and why I am here on Earth. I have remembered that by being selfish and taking care of self, I am better equipped to help others. I remember the power of love. I have happiness and joy in doing what I came to Earth to do. I am following my Soul Plan and so can you. I am who I am and can be nothing else!

How Did I End Up with Him?

Look at him,
Sitting over there,
He is so uncouth, so uncool.

Just look at him, sitting over there,
He is uncivilized, uncultured, unpolished and unsophisticated.

Look at him,
He is a Neanderthal,
And to boot, he's on Adderall.
He's not even that tall,
He looks so small.

Look at him,
He is unloving, uncaring, unforgiving,
He doesn't pay attention to me,
He listens not,
He's got that bald spot.

Just look at him,
Sitting over there in our chair.
How did I end up with him?

Do you know where you are going?

Is This the Girl for Me?

Is she the girl for me?
She is so very pretty.
I just don't know.
She is extremely flirty.
They say she used to stalk Smitty.
And she loves dresses that show a little titty.

Yet, she looks so good,
She is always dressed to a tee.
She takes extreme care of her hair.
Her skin is so fair.
Each day she shaves her legs with Nair,
But her legs are always open wide,
When she sits in a chair.

She has a small figure,
Word is she eats very little.
Maybe that's why her bones seem so brittle.

However, I must say she looked at me twice!
My friends say, she not very nice,

Her words always slice.
She speaks a lot of trashy phrases,
And her tattoos are in,
Some very weird places and spaces.
She doesn't like her father very much,
And she tends to speak ill of her mother,
She very rarely speaks high of her brother.
But she looks so good.
Not a hair out of place,
But she dates all over the place,
And she wants to screw,
In some strange open public spaces.

Is this the girl for me?

Chapter 4

Patricia's Original Life Map PSA

- To be in conflict with father and mother and remember to appreciate them. **Delayed with mother, Delayed & Completed with father**
- To obtain higher educational degrees. **Altered**
- To live in the Carolinas in North America. **Deterred, Altered**
- To travel to 22 countries. **Delayed, Pending**
- To not have any profession or secular work. **Grafted onto, not on original map. Completed**
- To struggle with self from age 2 to 34. **Completed**
- Purpose. To remember ability to see human auranic fields. **Delayed**
- Purpose. To master self-discipline. **Deterred**
- To question religion. **Ongoing**

- To meet soulmate and marry. **Completed**
- To continuously question marriage. **Grafted on to life map due to lower vibrations affecting the emotional being. Ongoing**
- To marry twice. **Altered**
- **Purpose.** To pen seven books to assist humanity. **Delayed, In Progress**
- To find spiritual self at age 9. **Delayed, Completed**
- **Purpose.** To be able to communicate with stones and crystals. **Completed, often unrealized**
- To bear 3 children. **Altered**
- **Purpose.** To become a healer. **Completed**
- To fully understand that women are equal to men and the leaders on Earth. **Deterred, Delayed**
- To remember not to carry stress in digestive. **Delayed, Deterred**
- To be in unconscious competition with mother. **Carryover from previous lifetime, carried over into daughter.**
- To question her mate's belief in her. (Fueled by whispers from the lower Angelic.) **Ongoing**
- **Purpose.** To find the gift of toning and other spiritual gifts. **Delayed, Deterred, Ongoing**

- To remember how to deal with the aging process. **Ongoing**
- **Purpose.** To open a spiritual center. **Deterred, Delayed, Completed**
- To overcome stubbornness. **Delayed**
- **Purpose.** To become a Reiki Master. **Completed**
- **Purpose.** To become a crystal surgeon. **Completed**
- **Purpose.** To feel disease in others. **Delayed, In Progress**
- **Purpose.** To find the prominent past life. **Completed**
- To complete A through Z in Soul Plan. **Deterred, In Progress**
- To live until the age 92. **Pending**
- **Purpose.** To reach Master level in life. **Delayed**

Patricia's Life

How would you feel if someone were to tell you that your life's purpose was to build a beautiful wellness center that would be well-known for the great work that is done there? You're no one special and have no background in health and healing. This is what happened to me many years ago. Hearing these words sparked something deep within my soul that I immediately knew was Truth.

In August of 2004 I found myself lost. My metaphysical teacher of many years taught me the basic metaphysical tools. Like a sponge, I couldn't get enough! Then came the time when I was ready for a new teacher. Liz had taken me as far as she could. A teacher can only teach what they know.

Advanced metaphysical teachers were, and still are, hard to find. So, I went to a channel that was recommended. This lady knew nothing about me, and here she is telling me my soul's purpose. The message about the wellness center was followed by a beautiful message from Archangel Gabriel that began: "We are grateful that you have returned to this path. You have followed this way many lifetimes. There will be things asked of you that will take courage. Always call upon your higher self and the Holy Spirit. They will help you find the courage to do as you know you should." I now knew my life had meaning and purpose.

Hearing these words sparked a flame within my heart that will never die. The message in its entirety is framed on a table beside my bed as a reminder. It has kept me moving forward, even when nothing appeared to be going right. Source/God comes to us in many ways. They plant ideas in our mind and send angels to work through people we know and don't know. The messages we hear inspire and guide us. They come through signs we see, songs we hear, and through people who don't even realize what they are saying is exactly what we need to hear. The guidance is always there.

Everything I have ever done in my career has prepared me for what I Am doing now. I have worn many hats—from an executive secretary working in areas of graphics, sales and marketing, public relations, and wealth management; to controller of an advertising agency and program coordinator of a national printing company—all without a college degree. The desk computer was fairly new when I was introduced to graphics. Software then was nowhere near what it is today. My nickname was the "chart queen," a result of the thousands of charts and drawings created in a few years' time. As an executive secretary working for this global company, I also learned the inner workings of upper management, public relations, sales and marketing.

One very special manager, Bruce, taught me what it was to be a true leader. Bruce was a visionary who founded a wealth management company. Bruce was able to see talents in people they didn't know existed, and he helped them to develop their gifts. He helped me develop my gifts of leadership and writing. Bruce also taught me how to take the high road should conflict arise. Bruce knew how to inspire and motivate people, and I admire him for the simple-yet-complex, good-natured person he is. Bruce has a heart of gold and desires to help people succeed, a very rare trait in management today. Source and the angels led me to him because they knew I would learn much from him, and learn I did.

My accounting experience came from a man I knew through Bruce. Jim asked me to be controller of his advertising agency—me who had no college degree and no background in accounting! Here I managed the entire accounting, human resources, life and health insurance plans, 401(k) plan, and payroll functions of the business. Jim trusted me, and I never let him down. Source and the angels led me to Jim so I could learn to take something that was in pieces (the accounting department was a disaster when I arrived!) and put it back together to run efficiently. I also wrote the office procedures manual, something that had previously been non-existent.

When the advertising agency sold, I worked for one of the top printing companies in the country. Here I managed and helped grow a $2.5-million account for the sales representative. This job fine-tuned my multi-tasking, writing, people, and organizational skills. I was a part of a team that developed the first successful print-on-demand program in the industry. In this complex, multi-faceted, high pressure job I used everything learned to date and more. Source/God and the angels led me to this job where I learned to accept, embrace, and adapt to change.

While I have no college degree, what I do have is common sense, a strong work ethic, excellent organizational skills, a desire to learn, and much life experience. No job is greater than another—whether it be the president of the firm or the janitor. Each role serves its purpose and is important; therefore, no position and no one in any position is greater than or less than another. Source/God and the angels are amazing!

So how did I get into healing? It was the result of many years of suffering from severe migraines (the result of stress). Nothing tried worked to release the migraines. So, in May of 2004 Source/God and the angels led me to a lovely couple who taught me Reiki. Eventually I was led to the lady who would teach me crystal surgery and the man who would teach me shamanism. Now my heart really sang! My journey has been both magical and mystical!

Growing up in a large family taught me to embrace diversity. Raising two children and being a grandmother of five, taught me compassion and a love I never knew existed. My wonderful husband and beautiful children keep me grounded while my amazing grandchildren remind me to take time to find joy in the simple things in life.

My home library consists of over five hundred books—all focused on spiritual and metaphysical knowledge. From these teachings I learned the message of a true messenger has depth and meaning, teaching how to live life. Any good teacher will teach you to look at yourself to bring about change. The answers lie within, not outside of the self.

Much misinformation is available today, especially on the internet. There are people who have a little bit of knowledge and think they know it all. There are those stuck in the ego and just want to "be" somebody. There are those who do not check to see where the information is coming from—inner guidance or fallen angels.

And there are those who find these people who are looking for the magic fairy wand (which doesn't exist) to take away all their problems so they don't have to do the work. It is important we use discernment to know the difference between that which is Absolute Truth (never changing) and that which is our perception of what truth is (always changing).

Everything I have ever learned prepared me for what I Am doing today. In April 2009 I founded White Dove Circle of Light and Love—a unique, one-of-a-kind wellness center for true healing of the mind, body, and spirit. Jim Wachter, Mary Benson, and Kay Brinkman have been by my side from the very beginning, and I Am grateful for their continued love and support. Source/God and the angels brought the four of us together to build this Center, just as Source/God led me to Linda Springer and Elliott and Diane Jackson.

A friend of mine moved to Texas in 2013 where Elliott and Diane Jackson were speaking at a local metaphysical store. Elliott and Diane are messengers of Source/God, and Elliott is a true channel for Source. Allen sent me one of Source's books channeled through Elliott. The autographed message inside the book read, "To whom much is given, much is required." Seeing this message sent a feeling that went deep into my core. I flipped through the pages of book and saw we were teaching the same information at White Dove Circle. I had to meet them!

My life took a turn when I met Elliott and Diane; meeting Source was a life-changing event. The way we met was Divinely orchestrated. Elliott and Diane were in Dayton in March of 2014. My mother was visiting so together we went to hear them.

Elliott and Diane arrived in time for the Group Channeling with Source that Friday night. Source/God channels through each of us every day, imparting ideas, wisdom, and guidance in our minds. All of the great masters in science, art, music, and dance have all channeled Source in their work. Whether we listen and follow this guidance is up to us.

Once the Group Channeling began, there was no doubt in my mind that Elliott was a true channel for Source. The look on his face, his mannerisms, and the tone of his voice all changed. Source told us many things that evening, but what stuck with me most was: "When you kill someone with a knife, you take their life. When you kill someone with your words, they take that with them throughout that life, and into the next, and into the next, until it can be resolved. It is by far worse to 'kill' someone's spirit with your words than it is to kill them with a knife." The message was profound and made perfect sense.

The following day my mother and I had private sessions with Source. The first session with Source is the same for everyone. Source reminds us that we are beautiful and gives us information to improve our family's dynamics and for own health and well-being—supplements we should take, juicing we should do, the type of exercise best suited for our body, etc. So that I would truly know it was Source, They reminded me of something I had done over thirty years ago that no one knew about except me and one other person. Society would have labeled me a "bad" person for what happened, so I purposely never shared what took place with anyone. Source then told me, "No one got hurt, you learned from the experience, and that's all matters."

Mom and I were so impressed with our sessions we called my good friend, Kay Brinkman, to tell her she had to come. In her session, Source told Kay that her marriage didn't work because she did not have a good relationship with her father. We marry someone just like our father to try to resolve that relationship. Source basically told her, "Your husband is not your father and you need to heal the relationship with your father if you want to have a successful relationship with any man." Another profound and meaningful message!

Mom, Kay, and I walked away that day knowing our lives had changed. We wanted more people to experience what we had just experienced so I asked Elliott and Diane to visit White Dove Circle the following April (2015). Everyone who came felt they had a life-changing experience too. Elliott and Diane returned again in October and have been coming to White Dove Circle several times a year since then.

In a private session (October 2015), Source told my good friend, Linda Springer, it was time to begin the wellness center and that she and I were to look for the space together. This was reiterated again in her April 2016 session. Source told Linda she was the key to finding space for the Center. Linda was flabbergasted!

How could she possibly be the key when she lived two hours away in Lima, Ohio?

Several years ago, we tried to purchase a house in Waynesville to start the Center, but the bank wouldn't give us a loan because White Dove Circle was a church and, therefore, not profitable. Banks are driven by profits; White Dove Circle is driven by service. Source later revealed in a Group Channeling the reason we didn't get the house was because the Community had not been supporting White Dove Circle wholeheartedly.

Source was right. It was time, and deep down we knew it. Linda was the key to finding the space. While driving around one day, we meandered into a business that rented commercial and residential property. Here we were told the "perfect house" had just been rented the week before. The owner's son-in-law, Dave, would let us know should something come up.

Linda and I went back a month later to check in with Dave. The owner of the business, Paul, joined us. Linda told Paul he reminded her of her own father. It wasn't long before we learned Paul's best friend of many years was

Linda's cousin who lived in Kentucky. Linda called her cousin, and the two men laughed and reminisced.

Paul got off the phone and mentioned he had a space we might be interested in and took us to see it. The building was originally a fire station, and then served as a fitness center and dance studio. At the time, it was being used as a warehouse. As rough as it was, it would be perfect for the Center! A contract was signed to rent the space, and a ribbon-cutting ceremony was scheduled for March 10, 2017. We had thirty days to get the space ready, and we had SO MUCH to do!

Source inspired the Community to come together. Dumpsters of trash were removed, mold was removed, and five coats of paint (three were primer) were needed to cover the fire engine red, jet black, and gray paint on the walls. Furniture and equipment were ordered. Soon the old, stagnant energy was transmuted into a loving, peaceful energy. We finished on time, and the space was beautiful! Linda and her husband eventually moved to the Dayton area to be an active part of the Center.

At the Grand Opening, Source asked me, "So how do you like this place WE found for you?" Yes, it was perfect! There were improvements yet to be made, but overall it had everything we needed plus room for expansion. Until we can build a magnificent Center of our own, this space will work just fine.

My life has had its fair share of ups and downs, heartfelt and heartbreaking moments, joy and sadness. Life is a journey. It can be an adventure, or it can be sedentary. Life is truly what we make of it. Through Elliott, Source has pushed me to be greater than I once was.

Since opening the Center, the Community of White Dove has grown and melded to work together as one, thanks to Source's push. Looking at the self is not for the faint of heart. If it were easy, more people would be doing it. The more you put into the journey, the more rewards you get out of it. And the rewards are well worth the journey!

Working with Source/God takes looking at the self to a higher level. Source pushes us in ways we do not always want to do. We may get angry with what Source tells us.

If we get angry, it is because we are hearing Truth—something we haven't wanted to hear. A session with Source is truly life changing—you can no longer be who you once were. Source can be firm when needed, and Source can be gentle. Children do not always listen to parents that are kind and gentle all the time. Tough love is often required. We tend to forget we are children learning lessons on this journey through life.

Follow the guidance Source gives you, and you will never be sorry. It is hard to get out of our own way, but when we do, life changes for the better because WE are better. If it weren't for Source, Elliott, and Diane, White Dove Circle would not be where it is today.

Elliott and Diane still visit White Dove Circle three times a year to do their work on behalf of Source/God. The Group Channeling is a favorite time of ours. In a private session, you may experience tears that release, anger at learning the Truth, and delight to learn what it will take to right yourself. If the advice is followed, change takes place and blessings flow.

Today White Dove Circle's experienced and effective healing practitioners work to help heal the mind, body, and spirit. White Dove Circle offers classes, workshops, and retreats for spiritual growth. We offer opportunities for ceremony, meditation, and world service. White Dove Wellness Clinic offers free healing for the financially-disadvantaged, and our Gift Shop offers items for continued healing, sacred books to assist in spiritual growth, and metaphysical items to enhance the spiritual journey.

White Dove Circle's healing practitioners join forces with practitioners from other states during "A Taste of Healing." This event includes healing sessions, workshops, a drumming circle, the Group Channeling with Source, and more. A Taste of Healing has grown from one day/twice a year (2009) to five days/three times a year.

A session with Source/God is truly a life-changing experience. If you cannot handle hearing the Truth, you are not ready for the Truth. The Community of White Dove and I are grateful for everything Source, Elliott, and Diane have done for us.

Chapter 5

Amy's Original Life Map PSA

- To be raised in a Jewish family. **Due to life in Germany as a solider in World War II**
- To Complete higher education. **Completed**
- Purpose. To question family's beliefs and seek spirituality. **Completed**
- To bear two children. **Altered due to choice of spirit (child), however, came as a pet**
- To meet and marry soulmate. **Completed**
- Purpose. To form a solid spiritual understanding. **Delayed, Ongoing now**
- Purpose. To write several books for humanity. **Deterred, Altered**
- Purpose. To be able to communicate with animals. **Delayed, In progress**
- Purpose. To be a natural healer. **Deterred, Delayed, In progress**

- Purpose. To be able to feel disease in people and animals. **Deterred due to self-doubt**
- To become a part-time screenwriter. **Delayed, Deterred**
- Purpose. To be able to communicate with the Angelic. **Deterred**
- Purpose. Battle and overcome depression. **Delayed fueled by lower vibrations**
- Purpose. To contract Cancer, accept, push away, heal. **Completed**
- Purpose. To assist others in dealing with cancer. **Far too often in limbo due to subconscious self-doubt**
- Purpose. To research spiritual matters, form own understanding of such, and become a Master to many students. **Deterred.**
- Purpose. To become a Reiki Master. **Completed**
- To complete A through Z in Soul Plan. **Deterred. In Progress**
- To live until the age 69. **Altered to age 89. Pending**

Amy's Life

It has been so far a good, typical life. In my teens and twenties, I didn't foresee opening my eyes to a much larger reality. I was a college graduate with no loans to pay, thanks to generous parents. Raised Jewish, but no particular interest in formal religion. I felt that religion was designed to limit your circle of friends and put some people above others. I was progressing in a marketing career, and eventually in my late 20's I met my husband Sean. Interesting side note – as he packed his things to move in with me, he showed me a wine cup that he kept coins in. It was inscribed with the name Kurt Kohlberg's Bar Mitzvah. I said, "That is my dad's cousin's name." Sean had gotten this silver cup when former tenants moved out of their rental property and left it behind, presumably it had been stolen. We checked with Kurt and in fact it was his cup and he was thrilled to get this piece of his history back. What a small world, maybe fate brought us together. Sean also likes to tell of getting a flash of our whole future together with me as soon as he met me. I think the universe was winking at me, but I didn't pay much attention to it yet.

We were able to purchase a condo, then a house, and occasionally we took vacations. In a few years our first and only child came along, a daughter named Brenna, who was named after our beloved dog Raven. Brenna means "little raven" in Gaelic. When Brenna was still a baby, Raven passed away in my arms and I was naturally devastated to lose her to cancer. A few months later I purchased a book by Lydia Hiby about animal communication. It seemed that she was able to telepathically communicate with animals both alive and passed away. I tried to become her client and reach out to Raven in the afterlife. She said she wasn't available but gave me the name of another qualified communicator. While I always had a passing curiosity about out-of-body experiences and aliens, I feel this marked the beginning of my real spiritual journey. The animal communication session took place over the phone and she said many things that seemed correct but the most amazing thing she told me was Raven said, "Thank you for the honor of naming your daughter after me." This was such a random and unknown fact that she couldn't have known. Raven also communicated that she would not be returning in another body, that she was busy doing things on the other side.

I dove into everything I could read about animal communication, took a weekend workshop to learn animal communication, and proceeded to learn more and more about the expanded world of metaphysical reality. I took some workshops at our local metaphysical store and began to read everything I could about the world beyond our five senses. At one point I went to a workshop with an artist who would draw a picture of a person's true being, mine was of a flower bud that had the potential to open. My curiosity was limitless about this subject and I would use my library card and my Amazon membership to read many books by authors such as Jane Roberts (Seth), Dolores Cannon, Michael J. Roads, Neale Donald Walsh, Lorna Byrne, and Pat Rodegast (Emmanuel) to name a few. I learned Reiki and proceeded to Level II, including a special course in

Animal Reiki. I hoped to have a future in doing Animal Reiki professionally someday. I always felt a pull toward animals more than people.

My daughter became a toddler and I switched to part time office work with mother's hours. Not very stimulating but it helped the budget. I did that for about 7 years and suddenly my mother developed stage 4 lung cancer and passed away very painfully 6 months later. My world was shattered even though I was certain that her soul lived on. I had some dreams that were vivid reunions with a healthy version of my mom (she seemed younger as well as healthy). I was very depressed, quit my job and decided to pursue a career as a dog trainer. It took several years to finish a training program that should have only taken one year or so. But my depression was holding me back.

Around this time, I was inspired to attend a workshop with Elliott Jackson at Circles of Wisdom bookstore in Andover, MA. What a wonderful way to continue my spiritual growth! I sat in the audience and learned about the first time he channeled Source. Then he channeled Source as we watched and listened. Ever since reading the Seth material many years ago, I hoped to be able to see this happen in person, and had seen some people channel, but this was a whole level above those others. I was one of the people to receive a gem stone and note that said "dream." On a tight budget, I didn't book a reading that year, but I did buy his book Sapiential Discourses Book 1 and read it cover to cover. I also reached out to Diane via email to ask a question about vaccines that I hadn't been able to ask during the class. She was nice enough to get right back to me with Source's answer that vaccines were indeed a gift from them, but to use them wisely (at least that is how I recall she answered, please do your own research on this subject, it is a touchy one).

I developed a severe case of IBS and tried many ways to alleviate the pain. Elliott and Diane were returning to New England in 2015 and I thought it best to book a session with Source to see if that could help. I also did a QXCI session with Diane. A few things happened that day. I had my session which felt truly like an honor. While he was channeling, Elliott/Source hugged me, and it felt amazing. Source gave me some tips about diet, supplements and I was to say out loud "I am healthy, and I am sending away any disease within my being." I also said out loud that I was thankful for the IBS because it was helping me grow and learn in this life. A month or two later, I finally returned to normal digestive health. I continued to stay in touch with Diane and Elliott because I signed on to receive a QXCI session once per month and we also began talking about the possibility of me preparing a script for a movie about Elliott and Diane's lives.

In 2016 I went to a breast thermography appointment expecting a completely normal test but was told to follow up with a mammogram because it didn't look good, and it turned out to be cancer which needed aggressive treatment. I was stunned, no family history and generally healthy, it couldn't be true. Source was consulted – surprisingly Source encouraged me to go ahead with chemotherapy. I had guessed they would have pointed me to fix it with diet, supplements, positive thinking. It seemed that I could do some good by interacting with the cancer center people, bringing in my ideas of minimal toxicity, more integrative ways to address the cancer and side effects. Throughout my cancer treatment and up through the present day, the QXCI healing sessions are helping me stay healthy on both the physical and deeper levels.

Also, I was treated to an advanced look at a chapter in The Sapiential Discourses Universal Wisdom Book III (now available for purchase) about reasons people get cancer. Source told me that I would be ok, that the cancer was for the purpose of "the acceptance of disease, by the person, which will cause the being to push the cancer out, heal oftentimes without any logical explanation, and assist others in doing the same in the future."

I noted in my life I was finding it hard to find friends who shared my interest in spirituality. Since I met Elliott, Diane and Source it has been easier to relax about that. Source will regularly put me in touch with other people that I can help by talking with them about my cancer experience or about dog training or anything that we might have in common. Source will also ask me and others to pray for someone who needs some special healing. It is a bit unnerving when Source calls on the phone unexpectedly. It's weird when you say "Oh my God" to yourself but mean it literally. I am so happy to be a part of such a wonderful community. I plan to go to the next gathering at White Dove Circle in April of 2019 to enjoy some members of this community in person.

As I bring my positive outlook to dog training, I feel that I am doing my part to heal others through helping them discover ways to communicate with their dogs in a peaceful way. In the past many trainers taught fear and pain methods, but today I am part of a huge new wave of trainers that use positive training. All the dogs I meet receive my love and I receive love back from them. I have joined with a woman who makes and sells flower essences to offer these natural-energy healing elixirs to dogs that have emotional problems. I hope to expand professionally into Animal Reiki and another holistic animal support.

I have learned so much from Source, including the fact that they know everything but most importantly that they are ok even after I didn't follow their instructions. You see, it is easy to ask, "What should I do?" and get an answer, but it is a lot harder to actually do it for a multitude of reasons, even when literally God told me it is in my best interest. Sometimes habits are very hard to break. Sometimes juice just doesn't sound appetizing plus it's kind of a pain to make it. Yet I know that they unconditionally love me no matter how much I fail to do. And I truly believe that with gratitude, kindness and good intentions, my life is ok, and every day is a new chance to be the best self that I can be. Remember to speak out loud to Source, They will hear you!

It's Been A Good Life!

It's been a good life,

Not too much pain and strife,

Although at times it felt like,

I'd been cut with a knife. Its been ok so far,

I've been able to buy cars,

My body doesn't have too many scars.

But, for a few years I was behind bars.

It's been a good life up until that date,

When I came face to face with some ill fate.

I went with those girls,

To that store,

Sandy pulled that gun,

Life after that for a few years was not too fun.

Maybe I should not have went with them,

Maybe they were not, after all, my true friends.

Chapter 6

Beverly's Original Life Map PSA

- Purpose. To be born into a large family. Completed. Due to previous lifetime of small family units, the spirit chose to come to a larger family. The imprint of the spirit in Beverly is so powerful that it caused the family it came into to expand far beyond its original, set boundaries.
- Purpose. To become a nurse. Carry over from a pervious lifetime. Completed
- To have internal strife from age 9 to 66. Almost completed.
- To marry twice. Altered
- To be tormented by lower vibrations from 6 to 23. Completed
- To be tormented by visions of doom from age 6 to 47. Altered
- To bear 3 children. Altered

- Purpose. To become a spiritual healer. Altered, Deterred, Completed.
- To marry at age 24. Altered
- To meet and marry soulmate at age 38. Altered
- To understand untrue spiritual information, age 21. Altered
- To overcome low self-worth age 23. Deterred, Altered
- To intertwine with 7 twin flames. Altered
- To meet 3 spiritual soulmates. Altered.
- Purpose. To become a master in 3 forms of spiritual healing. Completed
- Purpose. To remember the equality of all. Delay, Deterred, Pending
- Purpose. To open a spiritual center. Deterred, Pending
- To travel to 22 countries. Pending
- Purpose. To master meditation. Delayed, Altered, Pending
- Purpose. To become a Reiki Master. Completed
- Purpose. To become a Crystal Surgeon. Completed

- **Purpose.** To remember importance of prominent past life. **Completed**
- To complete A through Z in Soul Plan. **Deterred, In Progress**
- To live until the age 101. **Altered to 97. Pending**

Beverly's Life

I had loving Christian parents who became foster parents. They provided well for me in a middle-class life, in the Midwest, USA, despite their own personal anxieties. I was the oldest of 4 children (3 girls and 1 boy) of which my mother had all of us in just 4.5 years. We have remained fairly close, now even much closer after I spoke to Source through Elliott.

I was born feet first, 1 month early, at 6 lbs., 4 oz. My paternal grandfather said I was "born on the run". That is actually true. I have felt an urgency throughout my life that I needed to do something to help all of humanity. So even though I was silly when goofing around, most of the time I was pretty serious; searching, searching, searching!

At the age of 4, I looked out over the horizon from my 2nd story bedroom window on a farm and asked, "How did I get here?" And, "Where was I now?" At the age of 7, just before moving from the farm to the city, I remember seeing lots of "darkness" around me.

I had repetitive nightmares between the ages of 7 and 10; maybe longer. I cried much in school and lots of times would refuse to go to school. My mother did not know what to do with me. I felt afraid and that I was not good enough, yet still unbelievably shined in school. I remember at the age of 9 sitting in my grandfather's church pew, asking myself, and God, "Where are all the miracles (spoke of in the Bible) that Jesus did, today?"

At 15, I confessed Jesus as Lord at a rally in Tampa, Florida but knew there had to be "more". I kept searching, then got "baptized in The Holy Spirit" and spoke in tongues- "perfect prayer language", went to prayer meetings, and our family had many prayer meetings at our home. I read, researched and taught the Bible insights to many others through my young adult years. I loved the spiritual masters I read of in the Bible - Jesus, some of the prophets, King David's Psalms, and God, and I slept with my Bible for years, holding it close to my heart.

YET I was depressed as an adolescent, very afraid of boys. Even though I scored very high academically, I felt I could not survive in college, feeling depressed and confused. I had never had a job in high school. So, I went into the USAF instead as it was a more structured environment and would pay for my college as I wanted to be independent, away from my perceived father's control. I thought maybe I could be a nurse eventually, as being a doctor was too frightening a responsibility.

At 18, in the USAF, after Basic Training, my orders read to be trained as an Operating Room Technician, but I developed mono, and was put on light duty for 6 weeks helping a supply clerk. Then the orders changed after light duty for me to be a supplies clerk. I knew that was not right, as it did not match my capabilities listed on my USAF intelligence test. I cried and prayed to God.

I went to the chaplain who, as an officer, interceded to have the assignments NCO find me an opening in medical, which then was as a Radiology Technologist.

When in the USAF, I married the 1st time at the age of 19 to the first man I had sex with, mainly due to extreme home sickness and guilt about sex. This guilt about sex followed me most of my life. It was a sin to have sex before marriage and a sin to divorce. So, there I was, on the brink of Hell and not in my 20's yet! People thought I was weeping at my wedding for joy. NOT! I had originally planned to get my college degrees before marrying.

After honorably leaving the USAF with my new husband, I spent 9 months meditating daily for hours to try to let go of the emotional and spiritual confusion I felt in the Air Force and now being married. My parents lived where I went to college and we were close. My mother and I used to pray together often.

Then when I first went to college, at 21, I was on the Dean's List and The Honor Society and elected to Who's Who in American Junior Colleges. I felt wonderful but my husband was doing poorly in college. So, it was mixed blessings.

The first couple of years in college my clairvoyance and clairaudience abilities came out and Spirit was able to work through me to minister to some at the college. But that later dwindled as I stopped meditating to "Be Still and Know That I AM God." I got my Bachelor of Science in Nursing but in 5 years, not 4, as I took a year off after my 3rd year because I felt confused as I did not enjoy the nursing program and it seemed I really wanted to be a pastor or a psychologist. But I gave in and finished my last year of nursing school and got my RN anyway, just to be finished and have some way of supporting myself. I was about 26.

Then, about that same time, my 1st marriage ended after 7 years. I was not understanding how to love him or myself, having fallen prey to his verbal and emotional abuse and believing in him! He was not a villain. I judged him for our religious beliefs being different too and he was just young and lost like me in low self-esteem. We had no children. After the divorce I felt literally and physically like my right arm had just been torn off at the shoulder. It ached really bad for about a year.

I was frantically still searching and joined a biblical research group to get help trying to find out what was "wrong" with me and hopefully help humanity too. So, I connected with this group for 10 years until it collapsed. I moved to the Northwest. I did see and perform miracles. Really, as I look back, the angels were working overtime to help me during this very confusing time in my life when I was trying to put God first.

After 3 years, at about 30, I married a 2nd time but divorced 8 years later. I waited so long as, after 6 months, my dear husband started speaking most of the time like a very small child and would not get help. I felt so angry inside at our situation. We had no children. I did not believe I could be a good mother. Source later said that was not true. They said I was supposed to have had 2 children.

Within a year or so after the ending of my 2nd marriage, I was very depressed and sought help through a girlfriend's referral of a man that could help me drop my issues and learn not to recreate them again. That lasted 8 years associating with his group called "The Process". Later, people in this "group" realized he was using brainwashing techniques on us and doing other lower vibrational acts.

After my 2nd divorce and some shorter relationships, I finally married a 3rd time someone in that group that I was friends with for 4 years prior. But he changed immediately and treated me like his property. The friend I thought I had in him was gone. After 2.5 years we divorced traumatically as the group called "The Process" was falling apart and this 3rd husband's father had just died from cancer. For the first 1.5 years of our 2.5-year marriage, we made 6 trips back and forth to Florida to help his dying dad; then our business structure collapsed. We had bought a home that was lost in the divorce that was on 10 acres that I thought was perfect to be a healing center and school. I had taken some other training to have my own business as a Postural Alignment Therapist, to help people recover from pain, drug free. I was then studying Carolyn Myss's "Anatomy of The Spirit" at that time, feeling joy and writing more poetry, now out of the grips of that leader's influence. My husband did not like that he could not control me, and he tried drastic things, but Spirit was one step ahead. It felt like I was waking up out of a trance or something.

After this 3rd divorce, I was determined to just keep God-focused, spiritually focused, and took time off of work, quit nursing to meditate, pray and talk with God and write.

Then within a year I met a wonderful man 12 years older than me through a number of synchronicities, but about 4 years into our 8-year friendship he developed Alzheimers and asked me to stay living at his home until he got stabilized on his meds. During the same time period, my father was diagnosed with a cognitive stroke, so I was overseeing both of their care -only my dad was in Florida with caregivers there. I knew not to live with my dad due to our history of his perceived controlling personality.

After both my father and this northwest friend of Alzheimer's transitioned, I started a course long distance to enhance my plethora of healing modalities which originated in Florida. I began having many synchronicities in my life and was guided to move to Florida. Within 4 months I located a church there and saw a flyer about a seminar where Elliott Eli Jackson would be channeling Source at.

That morning before the seminar, I asked God to give me more hope. I had tons of energy flowing through me all day and was concerned I would not be able to drive. During the seminar, Source, through Elliott, handed me a packet with a word on it. It was the word "Hope", then the lady next to me exclaimed her name was "Hope" too! It was Source's tongue-in-cheek way to say they indeed had heard me that morning and were giving me "more" Hope!

*My greatest deterrent to following my Soul Plan was my low self-esteem with the idea that there was something terribly wrong with me. *

As a young adult, it led me to follow low vibrational male leaders in 2 different cults (their way was the only or best way) so I could get help to "fix" what I thought was "terribly wrong with me". (Crazy, I know now, as what was wrong with me was trying to follow them!) I also let other "friends" influence me through lower vibrations to be dominated at their whims to solve their problems, admire and build them up, because underneath I had lost sense of my own purpose. My purpose had turned into adopting their idea of being their "great friend" as I had also put them as more spiritual than myself and on a pedestal. Source later said that was not the Truth.

I did realize in middle age that all are equal and Christian people are not more special (or any type spiritual group) than anyone else. Twenty years ago, I started meditating again and I started feeling energy. So, I attended many types of energy healing and transformation classes through the years but, due to low self-esteem still, never stepped out to teach what I learned as something still did not seem right.

Now Things Being Set "Right"

Immediately after my first private session with Elliott channeling Source, I applied Source's proper information on how to release myself and others in our relationships together from any further karmic ties and free up all of us from these parts of our pasts. This process also helped me realize the gifts we gave each other in experiencing those relationships together of positive gains and lessons learned.

My vibration has been rising. I have new higher vibrational friends, and I met my Soulmate 2 years ago of which we are now in a healthy marriage relationship. Thanks to Source's encouragements, I practice the ancient art of Crystal Surgery, Reiki and other energy healing modalities to assist others in their wellbeing. I teach Spiritual Life Coaching as well as help others through spiritual life coaching.

I have started teaching seminars to small groups about stones and crystals and many other subjects and I will be doing video classes in the near future. I started writing a lot more, of which books are coming forth from my inspired poetry and prose.

Physically, from QXCI biofeedback reports, my cellular vitality has risen from 1 to 8 on a scale of 10 in less than 2 years. I no longer suffer from fibromyalgia, Epstein Barr or chronic fatigue and only need to take a few daily supplements and exercise regularly. I feel confident and accepting of who I AM and that there is nothing wrong with me and realize there never has been.

I may have been misled much of my life, but I am not wrong or a bad person for missing parts of my soul plan junctures in the past, as being back on my plan now is all that matters according to Source. Because and since I met my soulmate in my Soul Plan, I was able to travel with him on an Asian cruise recently and see amazing people and amazing places and wonders I would not have seen otherwise if I had not been led to meet Diane and Elliott and speak to Source.

Now I know for sure there is absolutely nothing wrong with me and never was…only lower vibrational influences to try to keep me from helping many others to remember they are OK too. Source has helped me understand how to have a successful male/female relationship and how to build healthy self-esteem through the knowledge channeled in Elliott's books and Source's sessions.

I no longer beat myself up when I make a lower vibrational mis-take. All I need to do is make higher vibrational choices in caring for myself to support my life in raising my vibration. I know now I am finally on my Soul Path doing my Soul Plan contract. I have much joy to teach and share from all that I have gained in the past 3 years of studying from Source's books to assist many. I also have my own seminars and books coming forth. There is great hope and peace in my life now with my soulmate that was part of my Soul Plan thanks to Source through Elliott and Diane's assistance.

Yes, there is hope for all!

Chapter 7

Eric's Original Life Map PSA

- To be born into a family considered above average financially. **Completed**
- **Purpose.** To have to overcome what is termed as being spoiled or feeling entitled. **Delayed, Deterred**
- To become a medical doctor. **Altered**
- To complete higher education by age 22. **Deterred**
- **Purpose.** To become a spiritual master. **Delayed, Pending**
- To marry at 26. **Pending**
- **Purpose.** To channel US at the highest apex. **Delayed, Pending**
- **Purpose.** To communicate with Elementals. **Delayed.**
- **Purpose.** To become a master. **Delayed**
- To travel to 13 countries. **Altered, Delayed**

- Purpose. To write 4 books. Deterred
- To father 4 children. Pending
- Purpose. To become a Reiki Master. Completed
- Purpose. To be able to send lower vibrations away from people, places and things. Delayed, Deterred, Pending
- Purpose. To find out about being an Indigo. Completed
- To find out important past life. Completed
- Purpose. To respect women. (Due to misinformation received from bloodline.) Delayed, Deterred, Pending

- To complete A through Z in Soul Plan. Deterred. In Progress
- To live until the age 85. Altered to 88. Pending

Eric's Life

I had been beaten up by life in my opinion. As much as I hate to admit it I am the product of a broken, dysfunctional family. Just the fact of not being raised all of my childhood in a totally happy family has affected me greatly. I was searching. I knew my answers were not at the bottom of a bottle or at the club, but I did not know where they were. After attending Florida State for a year and a half, I experienced a breakdown of sorts. The breakdown was on the spiritual, mental and emotional levels, which could do nothing but affect me physically. However, it was that breakdown that has led me to Source God and Self.

At the time of its occurrence I did not know what I wanted or where I was going. I was upset, frustrated, and had entirely too many questions with entirely too few answers. I was in pain, not just in emotional pain but spiritual pain. I did not know what to do. I would pray often, eat well and meditate. I looked in all the right places but found very few answers. I wished things were different. I wished the world was more peaceful, and most of all I sought my life purpose with fervency. I simply wanted to help people, but I did not know where to turn, where to look, or who to talk to. I knew an opportunity would present itself. I knew that the tides of life would swing in my favor once more, but I was upset! I didn't think I could have the woman I deserved, and I knew that I was not headed down the right path. I was at a loss but not without hope.

I began to seek out spiritual truths that held value. I began to chant to myself "I Love You All" every day. In all situations that I was faced with adversity or I was feeling troubled I would chant this, and then make my decisions. I realized that everyone was equal, truly, no matter what. I also began to understand that I had talents that others viewed as extraordinary, although I had not remembered how beautiful I was yet. I wanted the entire world to turn to each other and tell one another everything about themselves, like a giant list of things they had done. I believed that, if everyone did this, we would all see that our beliefs and behaviors really aren't that much different and that humanity at its root has a lot of commonalities. I believed that some of the things people have really held shame for would become eclipsed because their neighbor may have felt shame for the very same thing. I wanted everyone to see that they are equal! I could not stand anymore the thought of someone thinking they were superior because of their parents, or their finances, or their appearance. It no longer made any sense to me at all!

Then I began to pray. I wanted to help people. That was it, that was all. I would say "I am here on this planet, use me!" I wanted to be a part of something that really helped a lot of people. I wanted to uplift my fellow man and through this I felt I would find true happiness. Later I understood that this was my spirit coxswaining me as this was and is the case. I couldn't live a mediocre life, I wouldn't allow myself. In my mind, my measure of success became how many people would I help. That was what I set out to do and I was prepared to dedicate my life to whatever came my way.

Through my desire for change came forth the idea that there could be a peaceful world. We could all love and respect one another and there would be a balancing of what seemed unfair and unjust on Earth. There would be a rising up of sorts to eliminate human trafficking and the selling of people on Earth. I realized that more people needed love and that love would cure many of the illnesses that mankind suffers from.

When I heard the words of Source, I was forever changed. They spoke to my very soul. I knew immediately that I did not have the answers. I knew that Source knew what the answers were. I had more questions than I thought could be answered. I wished more than anything that someone could shed light on the many questions I had formulated. I wanted to have the answers so I could help, so I could heal. Ultimately, Source gave me answers to some of my questions and much more.

Chapter 8

Erin's Original Life Map PSA

- Purpose. To be born in a time where her physical attributes are consider beautiful or above most people on the planet and overcome vanity. **Completed**
- Purpose. To find out about being an Indigo. **Completed**
- To master financial responsibility. **Delayed, Deterred**
- Purpose. To question organized religion and find truth. **Delayed, Completed**
- Purpose. To become a healer. **Delayed, Deterred, In Process**
- Purpose. To communicate with Angels of high vibrations. **Delayed, Deterred**

- To allow 3 spirits to come to Earth through her. **Altered**
- To travel to 28 countries. **In Process**
- Purpose. To teach others about stones and crystals. **Delayed, Deterred**
- To meet and marry soulmate at age 18. **Altered, Delayed, Deterred**
- Purpose. To assist others in spiritually overcoming challenges in romantic relationships. **Started, Delayed, Deterred**
- Purpose. To become a Reiki Master. **Pending**
- Purpose. To be able to send lower vibrations away from places and spaces. **Delayed, Deterred**
- Purpose. To master self. **Delayed, Deterred**
- To complete A through Z in Soul Plan. **Deterred, In Progress**
- To live until the age 99. **Pending**

Erin's Life

I had a very "normal" childhood, if that is such a thing. I was brought up in a semi-religious household. I say semi-religious for my immediate family did not impose any specific beliefs upon me but my extended family was very conservative and very involved in the Baptist community. I can recall certain times questioning my grandparents when certain ideas of exclusion or persecution of other beliefs, people, or ways of life would surface within the teachings. None of it seemed to make sense to me and this whole idea of a God who judges and condemns didn't sit well with my childhood innocence and clarity on the world. I always created my own path and challenged conventional ways of thinking but didn't necessarily have a direction to explore my thoughts further or expand upon my beliefs.

As I continued through adolescence, trying to navigate the world on my own, caught up in self-deprecating and demeaning thoughts of self, I allowed the world to tell me I was never enough, and I believed it. I carried this into each relationship I would enter and eventually these relationships would become the "purpose" that I designed for my time here on this Earth.

The first time I spoke with Source was in 2013. Looking back, I really can't say what in the world prompted me to actually take the leap of faith and speak to Them through Elliott. I had never done anything remotely close to this before. Obviously, in hindsight, I understand the bigger forces that were at work. Nonetheless, I went on this day, practically stuttering with insecurity, and felt an immediate calm wash over me the instant Source came through. I always describe this moment to people as the clearest indicator of the absolute truth and love held within Source's words and teachings. There are some things that are undeniable in life. That moment was one of those times.

For many years I would see Source sporadically, more just looking for answers in the moment, ways out of predicaments, or solutions to "problems" I saw in my life. I occasionally listened to Their advice and saw whatever They told me unfold before my eyes. However, this is where these sessions with Them ended. I did not take Their advice to start taking ownership of my life and my relationship, refusing to become the leader of my romantic relationship which so desperately needed me to be just that. All the while I suffered, thinking I knew better but playing the victim.

There was one particular session with Source over the years where They advised me not to make a particularly big decision in my personal life that I felt I had no choice but to make. Rather than having faith in what They were telling me, I continued with my decision out of fear. This one decision has altered the course of my personal life greatly and a short while later I had my very first child in an emotionally challenging situation. While I never could have envisioned my life going the way it did, I was able to learn a lot from this situation and ultimately unconditional love for of course, my child, even her father, but most importantly myself.

Finally, I was at a point in my life where I started to put myself first. Ironically, being in the most selfless role of my life as a mother taught me that for everyone to thrive, it had to begin with me. I began taking care of myself and watching my vibration rise. I would occasionally talk to Source and They finally deemed it time for me to begin my path helping others. I began undertaking the path of becoming a Life Coach as well as studying to become a Reiki Master and understood both roles were absolutely not to be taken lightly. This newfound responsibility to others made it transparently clear that I had to keep my vibration at the highest possible level in order to be able to uphold my end of the bargain as their practitioner and serve them for the highest good.

For the first time in all the years of speaking to Source, I finally began following their advice on personal care. They will always tell you "to whom much is given, much is required" and the "self-care" routine, if you will, is an absolute must, there's just no way around it. I began making my juices sometimes, working out occasionally, meditating daily, and saying my "I AM" proclamations when I found the time. After a couple months of this I realized how much better I felt when I followed these steps as I should and, through experience, that all would work out. I began to understand that I should always wish to be the best that I can be. Additionally, why would I ever choose to feel or be less than my best? Yes, each individual piece of this routine I had adopted could be thought to be life-altering, but the combination of all of them is unequivocally and irreversibly life-changing. All of a sudden, it dawned on me and I understood what being the creator of my life meant. All these years I had heard and read sentiments and teachings about being the creator of my life, not just from Source, but many different avenues and finally it all made sense. It's interesting that as I began to do my I AM's day in and day out without fail, I began to see them all appearing in my life. I always joked that I quite literally became a walking, talking I-AM. As soon as this realization came about my creator-ship, I immediately saw the link to the 15th I AM, which is "Freedom of Choice." I realized that, being the Creator that I was, I had the full and complete ability to CHOOSE the life I wanted. No more playing the victim, no more choosing to feel sub-par, no settling for less than I deserved in not only relationships but in life, and no more floating aimlessly through this lifetime not serving the PURPOSE I came here for. I began to carry this idea of having a choice with me throughout every single day and, more specifically, every single moment. I had hundreds, thousands, of opportunities to choose what was not only in my highest good but in the highest good for all others around me. This realization and implementation into action has catapulted my life onto a course I could not have dreamed of coming to me.

The avenues and doors to consciousness and personal growth that burst open for me since taking the driver's seat in my own life have been astounding. Everything seems to open up for me just as I need it to, and I am brought to whatever experience or opportunity I need. While "life" is still "life" in this human experience, and emotions and certain experiences can sometimes be seen as hard, I face everyday setbacks or pitfalls with a resounding base of faith and purpose.

Affixed

She was affixed on what should be,
Instead of what could be.
She was attached to what might be,
Instead of what will be.
She was chained to what happened,
Which caused her glasses to be blackened.
She was imprisoned in the past,
Which brought about,
The inability to complete a simple daily task.
She was stuck in the now,
Petrified from the future.
Which made it impossible,
For happiness to come sooner.

Chapter 9

Billy's Original Life Map PSA

- Purpose. To be born in the United States of America (related to past life as shaman). Completed
- To break the cycle set by father. Delayed, Completed
- To marry twice. Pending
- Purpose. To question everything. Ongoing
- To become financially secure. Delayed due to non-belief in self, Pending
- Purpose. To overcome fear of public speaking. In Process
- Purpose. To become a healer through the sound of his voice. Delayed, Pending
- To teach Tantric Sex. Grafted onto plan, Deterred (due to fear)

- Purpose. To become a master in 5 healing modalities. Delayed
- To visit all Earth's Vortexes. Grafted onto plan, In progress
- Grafted on Purpose. To write a book on vortexes. Pending
- Purpose. To fully understand Vortexes and Portals and become one of Earth's authorities on such. Delayed
- Purpose. To teach Spiritual Awareness. Delayed, Deterred
- Purpose. To become one of OUR true Shamans. Delayed, Deterred
- Purpose. To find out the most important past life connected to present life. Delayed, Deterred
- Purpose. To become a Reiki Master. Pending
- To complete A through Z in Soul Plan. Deterred, In Progress
- To live until the age 93. Pending

Billy's Life

My interaction with Source started about a year and a half ago. Prior to meeting Elliott, I always had a knowing there was more to life than I was led to believe. I was raised in a hardworking, loving family and taught to always work hard, be honest with my words, and to come from a loving place. I always had a void in my life. I worked hard, met a loving woman, got married and had two beautiful girls. I did as I was taught, to work hard and provide for my family, just like my father did. The thing was, I didn't like the person I had become. I was becoming like my father. Although he was a provider and hard worker, I didn't have much of a relationship with him due to his career and life choices.

I found myself working long hours and not happy where I was with my relationship with my family. I had become a people pleaser and even though I was making everyone happy, I wasn't happy. My relationship with my wife and kids were suffering from the long hours at work. My fifteen-year marriage wasn't what it once was, and we were growing apart. I felt like I was losing it all and losing my self-identity. I was lost!

I decided at the last minute to take a weekend getaway with some friends. It was on this trip that I realized I don't do anything for myself, let alone love myself. I was working fifty plus hours every week and drinking my weekends away trying to escape the "void" in my life. During this trip I realized there was more to my life. When I got home from my trip, I knew I had to change things. For the past five years the loving relationship with my wife had changed to a constant battle. We loved each other but no longer had a companionship. We talked about separating, but due to the young age of our children we decided it would be best to try and live together and make it work. Then I realized I could no longer go on living and fighting under the same roof. It was taking its toll on all of us.

Prior to leaving for my trip I had reached out to a friend who was a holistic healer. She shared some interesting things with me about myself and family. After our conversations it seemed like doors started opening with answers. A friend from grade school reached out to me and told me I needed to contact Elliott and have a session with Source. I remember the day clearly, a day I will never forget!

I have always been a seeker of truth and believe me, my first session I went in eyes wide open not knowing that this day was going to change my life as I knew it. We talked about things that I never spoke about with anyone pertaining to me, my life, and the crossroads I was encountering. I did more listening than speaking, as I was in awe by the words Source spoke. Without going into detail, after I had spoken to Source, I sat in that empty, dark parking lot on that cold winter night just thinking. Could all this be real? Could all this be true? I knew in my heart it was, but in my mind, I questioned everything. I knew in my heart I could no longer go on living in a loveless marriage. I didn't want my children to think this was how a loving marriage between two people was supposed to be. I sat down and told my wife I wanted to move out and give her the space for both of us to have some time and try and figure out who we were and becoming. We both needed a break no matter how hard it was going to be on us. I knew it would be best for all of us and I couldn't bear the stress and anxiety it was putting on all of us. This was one of the hardest decisions I had to make in my life, as I felt like I failed myself and everyone that was involved in our families.

From that day on, the flood gates open for me. Synchronicity was everywhere I looked. Source told me to start praying out loud and meditate, to listen for and hear the answers I was seeking. One of the hardest challenges was to look myself in the mirror and tell myself "I Love You"! As easy as this sounds, it wasn't that easy. I hated who I had become, all that I could see in the mirror was a person who let his wife down and failed his two girls. I hated myself and the person I became. Now I was supposed to look at myself in the mirror and tell myself "I LOVE ME"! It took me a few weeks, then I noticed when I did this I would blink or look away. I forced myself to look myself in the eyes and repeat the words, "I LOVE YOU"! No blinking. No looking away. I would focus on my eyes in the mirror, looking in at my soul, and repeated the words, "I LOVE YOU"!

I had no idea how things were going to work out. The fear of the unknown took over. I started praying, meditating, reading, and absorbing more. My thirst for knowledge and my desire to figure out my soul's purpose was driving me.

I joined the gym and started to challenge myself in ways I had never done before. I met a yoga instructor and started taking yoga. I met a physical trainer and started training with him. I started doing for me again while healing and trying to love me for the person I was, exactly at that moment in time. I reconnected with a high school friend of mine, a financial planner, who helped me regain my financial stability. I found a beautiful apartment not far from my girls. From this point forward, everything started to unfold like it was all planned out. During this time, I started reading Elliott's books, *The Sapiential Discourses*, Volumes One, Two and Three. I started reciting the I AM mantras from the books. Everything I read just seemed to fit and make perfect sense.

This is when things really took off for me. I had this desire to seek out the truth. The answers I had always had, but I didn't trust myself enough to believe in them. I started traveling to places that called out to me. My friend from high school told me about a place that I never heard of, Sedona, Arizona. She told me I needed to go to Sedona and visit the energy vortexes there. She told me she was going the following week and asked if I would like to join her. I jumped at the opportunity and made the week-long trip.

There was something about Sedona I never experienced before in my life. Everything felt so much lighter, so much easier. The long hikes throughout the energy vortexes made me feel alive again. Emotions started to come out, ones that I had pushed down and away for so long, emotions that I didn't understand at the time, but now it all made sense. The isolation from the real world as we know it was what I needed. I needed to let go of my past. I needed to understand that I'm exactly where I'm supposed to be right now in my life. I realized I need to start trusting more, trusting myself and trusting others. I started loving me again and the person I was and becoming.

When I returned from this trip, I knew right then and there I needed to get back to Sedona. I didn't know how it would happen, but I needed it. Every day I would pray and meditate. I would follow my routine of waking, repeating my mantras, looking in the mirror and telling myself "I love me, I love myself, and I love the person I was and the person I am becoming." During my meditations, I would think about Sedona and the love I had for this special place. That's when the call came in.

My friend was taking a business trip back out to Sedona. She asked if I would like to join her. I couldn't believe that this was really happening. I gave gratitude to Source and the Universe for the trip that was unfolding. Could this really be happening to me? I knew I had to get back out to Sedona. It was calling me. During this trip, it came to me that I had to bring my girls out to Sedona to experience what it was I was feeling on these trips. I knew I had to bring them out there to help them heal and to heal our relationship.

I planned a trip with my friend to take my kids out to Sedona over holiday break. It was the most amazing trip for all of us. I took my girls on long hikes through the vortexes. During these hikes all the emotions that were deeply pushed down in all of us started to come out...joy, happiness, sadness, fear, and love. Some of the trails were challenging but, on each hike, it was as if a layer was being healed. By the end of the trip, I knew this was where I was supposed to be with my girls. It was the healing I needed to do with them. I needed to let them know I was going nowhere and would always be there for them. I was their father and their souls picked me on their soul journey, as well as my soul picked them too. The love I had for them was unconditional. I wanted them to know I would always be with them. Our bond and trust for one another had grown so much for one another on this trip.

When I returned home from this trip, I received a call from Elliott. He stated that Source told him he wanted me to give an hour-long speaking presentation. Prior to this call, I attended a seminar on "Finding Your Soul Purpose". The speaker, Robert, said, "You will know what your soul purpose is when it comes into your life and scares the crap out of you." I laughed at the time, but now sat with the fear of getting up in front of a group of people and to talk about my life journey with a complete group of strangers. This couldn't be happening to me.

That's when synchronicity was screaming at me, it was so apparent. I became friends with a healer in Sedona. She sent a text to me that night and told me she had a friend she wanted me to meet. He is a speaker and gives lectures for a living. "No", I thought at first. I don't give lectures or speak in public. That is when I realized what Elliott wrote about. We all have freedom of choice. I can say no and go about on my way, or I could trust and believe in myself and face my fears. I chose to travel to Ohio and attend the weekend long event.

When in Ohio, fear completely came over me. What was it I was going to say to these people? I had no idea what I was even doing there. That is when Source contacted me and told me it would be alright, to trust. I went into the speaking engagement with little notes and trusted it was all going to be perfect and it was! After this event, I started to gain the confidence in myself again, to trust me and to believe in myself after all the years of doubting me.

As my journey continues, I have learned many valuable lessons and continue to grow each day. Source has taught me that we all hold the answers we seek. Believe in yourself as you are God, you are Source. We are all one. Treat everyone as they are you, and they are you. Love yourself as you are, you are exactly where your supposed to be right now at this very minute. Trust and follow your heart. If you listen to your heart and quiet your mind, you will never choose the wrong path. Breathe, relax and don't take yourself so seriously. Life is a beautiful journey, so enjoy it. There will be good days and there will be bad days but, know, we are all creators. We choose every morning what direction we want our day to go. Choose love and choose to be happy. Believe me, that is what will happen. Is the journey easy? That's up to you to decide how you want it to go. Know in your heart you hold the key to all the answers you seek. Trust yourself and your life will never be the same! Peace and Love.

Chapter 10

A Look into Some Soul Plans

WE will here give insight into some other **actual** Soul Plans of people on your home, your planet, your Earth; how they were, and how they turned out after remembering who they were and why they came into the encasement that they dwell or dwelt in. WE will not be providing their Maps as WE did previously with the other eight encasements. WE will, however, explain some of their challenges and how they overcame them, some of their (what many of you may consider) tragedies and how they walked through them and came out the other side to fulfill their personal Soul Plans. WE will also offer up some who did not remember who and what they are, refused to change and, so, reaped the consequences of such.

John W. – In John's plan was for him to Minister to Others. John grew up in an Irish household in Boston,

MA. His father was a hard worker, not home often. When his father was home, he was abusive to his wife and his children. John saw his father beat his mother and verbally abuse her often. John developed a resentment with his father for the way he treated his mother. John developed a resentment with his mother; he thought her weak. Consequently, even as he stated he hated his father, he began, as he grew older, to treat women in the same manner as did his father. He met his soulmate, unknown to him due to his vibration at the time. John stayed married for five years and had two children and he abused them physically and verbally.

John went to mass with his family. He could not understand how WE could love his father, because of his actions. John was bitter, angry and, to say the least, very frustrated. John's father drank a lot, in turn, so did John as he matured. One night, while driving home from a bar, drunk, John was in and the cause of a fatal accident in which a mother and her son were killed. John's car flipped over several times and he punctured his lungs. While in the hospital recovering, one of John's Angels whispered to him – "It is time to be that which you were meant to be." From that moment on, John picked up the joy of completing his Soul Plan. John stopped drinking and stopped abusing his family. John began to visit a holistic center. John started to take full responsibility for his actions. John had an epiphany. He saw that his mother and father were as they had become because it was all that they knew. It was a way of life that they were shown. John began to have more conversations with his mother and father and formed a most loving relationship with them before they transitioned. John became happy. John began to cherish his leader, his wife, and to honor his children and himself. John began practicing touch healing, became a master, and now he teaches such. John also speaks to the youth that he encounters. John is a minister of OURS. John is holistically whole and fulfilling his Soul's Plan. The universe is happy!

Sara J. – In Sara's Soul Plan was to contract Cancer and die. Sara grew up mostly in Pensacola, Florida in the United States of America. Her father was in the United States Air Force and she had the opportunity to travel to Turkey and Germany, becoming quite proficient in speaking the German language. She went to good schools and received what you would consider to be good grades. It was a loving household consisting, most of the time, of her, her mother and two brothers. WE say most of the time because of her father's occupation. Yet, while he was at home, her family spent good quality time together. Sara went on to receive a bachelor's degree and began to work as an office manager in a small but flourishing construction conglomerate. Sara met her soulmate, married, allowed two wonderful spirits to enter your planet's atmosphere from her womb. She was successful, her husband was successful, and all was well.

One day, while getting dressed for work, she noticed a lump on her right breast, and she did not inform anyone. After a while, however, the lump began to tax on her mental. Sara decided to let her husband know and visit a doctor. The diagnosis came to be breast cancer that had begun to spread throughout her entire chest cavity. Sara asked the doctors what could be done. She was advised that the cancer had spread too much for anything to be done. Sara prayed to US and asked for the strength to handle that which had occurred. Sara accepted, what many thought to be, a dilemma with grace and gratitude. Sara accepted she had had a wonderful life, marriage, career, and a loving family. During meditation, it was revealed to her that it was within her soul plan to assist her mother, father, mother-in-law, father-in-law, brothers, husband and children with acceptance and compassion. Sara began to let all know not to be sad for her, and not to grieve too long for she had come and completed that which was designated within her soul plan. Many could not understand her appearance of peace and tranquility. However, she would always inform them that life happens as it does. Sara accepted minimum medication for pain and did transition in a peaceful manner. She was a positive role model for all as set forth within her soul plan. Of course, her spirit returned to US and is, in fact, now, due to her disposition during her encasement, returned in the form of a child in Detroit, Michigan. This child will exhibit peace and calm all the days of its life and will be a shining example to all that come within close proximity to its being. This kind of return is possible on your planet and plane if one accepts the Soul Plan that their being set forth long ago and far away.

Raji B. – In Raji's Soul Plan was to be a Shaman. Raji grew up in a Muslim household in the city of New York. Raji, as a child, was always a seeker and a searcher of answers. Raji believed in the Koran as it is written. However, Raji could not understand the divide between certain fractions of Muslims in other countries if, in fact, they were the Muslims that they professed to be. Raji began to have prophetic dreams just before 9/11. These dreams were always about a medicine man. Raji began to investigate Shamanism. He began to study and take courses and classes on Shamanism. Raji did a sojourn to Mexico and visited the great temples of past civilizations. Raji began to teach Shamanism and he became a master. Today, Raji is respected and admired for his ability to see inside the souls of men and women. Raji is fulfilling his Soul Plan. Now please understand that, due to his ethnicity and where and how he grew up, to many, he would seem to be the least likely candidate to become a Shaman. Yet, WE tell you, as laid out in his Soul Plan, Shaman he is and Shaman he shall be.

Brenda W. – In Brenda's Soul Plan was to have Eight Children and Marry Three Different Men. Brenda grew up in Liverpool, England in a family that did not have many means. As she grew, she became quite flirtatious with the opposite sex and did have a child at the age of fifteen. Brenda formed a resentment with her first child for coming too soon, in her mind. Nonetheless, she married the father of the child, divorced within two years, remarried, had four children within the span of seven years. Then in the ninth year, in the marriage that WE mentioned, she had another child. Brenda divorced her second husband, remarried nine months later, and had two more children, which brought the number to eight. Brenda began to frequent a healing circle, and during the course of one of the sessions, she began to accept that all that had occurred to her was for reason and purpose. She began to understand that her Soul Plan involved finding love, losing love, heartache and pain. Yet all of that produced the eight wonderful children that she has never spoken an ill word to. From the time that she was little, she intuitively understood that all are beautiful in the eyes of God. WE are grateful that Brenda accepted her Soul Plan.

Clyde D. – In Clyde's Soul Plan was to Travel the World Helping the Poor. He always knew it. Some just know their place in the world on your planet from the beginning, Clyde was one. Clyde was born in 1980, in what you would understand to be as Southern California, to a family of meager means. All his life he was quiet and reserved, and he knew he must help the poor. When he was little, he would give his toys away after playing with them one time, if at all. After graduating high school, Clyde joined the Peace Corp and has since traveled the world. Clyde is now comforting and assisting the poor. This, WE tell you, was all within the Soul Plan for his encasement. Some Soul Plans are not as intricate or as complex as others. Some are simple and straight to the point. Such was Clyde's. What about yours?

Diane C. – In Diane's Soul Plan was to be an Intuitive. When Diane was a small child, she would talk to her friend. Yet no one else could see her friend, but she did. She would tell her mother of things that she had no way of knowing at such a small age. She would always talk to US. Many thought her to be off a bit. Even her mother and father did not believe her. Diane knew her friend was real. She could see into the parallel world. And she continued to speak to the Angels all the time. She would be given information to help people. None of the information provided to her was ever of a low vibration. Diane, to this day, speaks to the spiritual world. She does not speak to the dead. That, of course, is not possible. Diane reads Tarot Cards for a living and is helping to guide many to higher levels of vibration. WE are happy!

Cindy R. – In Cindy's Soul Plan was to be a Prostitute and, later, become an Advocate for Abused Women. Cindy was raised in Las Vegas; she never knew anything but prostitution. Her mother was a prostitute and her aunts. She was a real hustler. She knew intuitively that women are the leaders of planet Earth, and she used this information in a negative fashion to harm herself and others. Yet, inside, she knew that her good looks and smile was for much more than pleasing men. She covered up her disdain with drugs and tried to stay in a stupor as much as she could. Cindy experienced many overdoses, wishing she could leave your world. But each and every attempt she made to take her life failed. Why? It was not in her Soul Plan. Cindy was at the end of her rope, she did not know what to do. Then one day she walked into a metaphysical shop, not by chance WE tell you, and her life changed forever. A wonderful lightworker saw the glimmer of hope still left in her eyes. The worker began to talk to her about OUR love for all of you. She explained that – All is forgiven! She pointed Cindy to a protection stone for her to carry. Cindy started to carry stones for protection while she would work the streets. Cindy started to read about stones and how they are of a higher consciousness. She began to pray to US out loud and ask for a change of heart. She lifted her very vibration WE tell you. She stopped selling her body and began to take better care of herself. She stopped eating meat and worked out four days a week.

OUR Cindy began to speak out for abused women. She began to help them; she would assist them in forming escape plans to leave their abusers. She started to assist them in seeing that the only way to help the abusers was to draw a line and leave them. She explained that leaving them could very well be the turning point for the abusers as well. Cindy helped them to remember that you can do whatever you desire to, and that you need no one's approval, except your own. Cindy totally changed her life, she began to understand that she deserved the best and, therefore, she started to tell all other women the same. She began to demand respect in a non-aggressive way. She took the time and wrote letters to all the men that had abused her on the streets. She wrote letters to all in her past. Cindy read each letter out loud and burned them, thus releasing her past. Cindy was, unknown to her, following her Soul Plan. She now began to understand that everything happens for a reason. Guess What? You can too. Then, one day, while helping a woman and her child leave an abusive husband and father, who was not home at the time, they heard his car. The father, whom was under the influence of lower portions of US and not remembering who he was, decided to come home early. Once in the home, he encountered Cindy and his family in the process of leaving him. He pulled out a pistol and shot Cindy in the head. Cindy died carrying out her Soul Plan. What do you think of this?

Pierre P. – In Pierre's Soul Plan was for him to Dislodge Lower Vibrational Entities from places and spaces. He intuitively knew this, yet he ignored it and fell into a state of low vibration. Pierre began to associate with individuals that call themselves Masters of the Darkness. Pierre bought into and participated in many dark rituals as you understand the term, allowing lower portions of US to influence his actions and behaviors. Consequently, Pierre went insane, as you understand the term, and currently resides in a mental institution. Pierre has not and will not follow his original Soul Plan and, unfortunately, will experience reincarnation to remember, once again, who he is and the majesty of his being.

Billy E. – In Billy's Soul Plan was Never to Speak. Billy was born in Huntsville, Alabama, and from the time he was born he has never spoken a word. Yet, Billy knows it was and is in his Soul Plan. He is proud of who he is. Billy understands that he is a gift to all. His gift to all is to practice patience and pay attention when dealing with him. Billy is loved and respected by all whom see his face. WE are grateful for him and his acceptance of his gift to humankind and his Soul Plan.

Hector Z. – Hector's plan included in it the provision for him to be an Electrical Engineer and later Assist Others in Healing with his Hands. Hector was very bright and was bullied as a child in school. Hector began to run with a gang of youths his age in Los Angeles, California. Hector stopped going to school and dedicated himself to the gang and the selling of drugs and guns. Hector was walking one day and passed a metaphysical shop; his spirit pushed him gently inside of such. Once inside, Hector could feel the love and positivity and he loved it. He informed his friends of the shop and the feeling that he felt when in the presence of the crystals. His friends, whom were under the influence of lower portions of US, due to them not loving themselves and thinking that they needed others' approval, just as Hector felt, did inform him that it was magic hocus pocus bullshit. Hector trusted his friends even though his spirit was trying to change his mental view of self and his world.

Hector decided to never go back into the shop and to continue this way of life. Hector robbed a gas station, as a dare from one of his so-called friends, and was killed in the process of such. Sadly, he never fulfilled his purpose and Soul Plan. And, the people that were to benefit from his gift of touch healing could not do so. The good news is that the spirit, that dwelt in Hector, has returned to your planet in another child in the state of Utah, and will have the opportunity to fulfill the Soul Plan set forth long ago and faraway.

Edward S. – In Edward's Soul Plan was for him to be Very Intellectual, have a Quick Sharp Mind and a Sharp Tongue. He was to be a true Starseed, rebellious, and run away from home at the young age of fourteen, hitchhiking across country. It was for him to be liked by many and misunderstood by most. His behaviors caused him to drink, drug and engage in risk-taking activities. He did so most of his younger years. He was to marry and allow two spirits to come to Earth in the form of his offspring. He was to divorce and become bitter, frightened and angry due to him forgetting how wonderful he was and allowing lower portions of US to influence his actions. He became a shadow man.

Then one day his marvelous spirit surged to the front of his being and led him to a friend and spiritual mentor, whom, by the way, was his friend and spiritual mentor in a previous lifetime on Earth. He surrendered to self and stepped out of the shadows. He then began a most intriguing journey into self and today he is a guide to many lost souls as was he. Now, he is on the verge and in the final stages toward receiving the true happiness that eluded him for many a year. However, he still displays great resistance and must overcome judgmental behaviors. He is a servant of humanity and US, yet anytime he does not display his gifts in a positive manner, there have and will continue to be lower vibrational consequences.

Coretta S. – In Coretta's Soul Plan was to be Autistic and to Create Beautiful Works of Spiritual Art. Coretta always played by herself and, if interrupted, would throw fits. Her mother and father did not know what to do. She would put strange images on the walls in the house whenever and wherever she could. WE tell you, her art, or what her parents thought meant nothing, sells for much money today. And her art brings peace to the souls of many. Her parents took her to, what they were told, were specialists on the matter. They (specialists), of course, knew nothing about how deal with her, WE will say, condition. Yet, WE inform you that the **cause** of what many of you consider to be her disorder is known to US and to those with the gift of autism, as set within their very Soul Plan. A direct cause, as you say, is not and will not be understood on a medical level for many years to come. Yet your kind will understand autism on a deeper level before the year 2087. From working with Coretta and those like her, you will be able to identify the portion of the human brain that stimulates such behaviors. **However, once again, not now!** In Coretta's case, her autism did not begin until around the physical age of three. This is what many in the medical and mental professions believe. WE inform you that it began the second her physical encasement exited the womb in which she laid. Additionally, Coretta and those like her do not suffer from developmental disorder either. **It is a gift.** Coretta has and never has had any connected impairment in social skills.

Coretta has the gift of - **communicating with her others in a different manner** from that which, most on Earth, are accustomed to. WE inform you here that Coretta and those like her have a total awareness. Coretta is clearly involved, in more ways than you know, with everything and everyone around her. Those around her just have to listen and watch. If one of you pays close attention to her and those like her, you will see the wonder in them. Yes, indeed, it was within her Soul Plan to take on the attributes attached to this form of your species from the very start of her life. Coretta has always been aware of the feelings of others. Yet, within her Soul Plan, was and is for her not to let others know this through any sort of verbal or non-verbal communication. Coretta and all others, that are of the same makeup as she, decided to assist their others on Earth with – **acceptance, patience, tolerance, and compassion.** It is who she is in this lifetime. All of things that stimulate Coretta and those like her are external. So, **Coretta has remembered** to let all know when they meet her of the wonders that she sees and feels in everything.

Coretta's outward displays or outbursts are teaching tools for those around her. Her ability to not care for herself, as your kind thinks she should, helps others to receive the gift of love that she is offering to them. Be it known now to all of you that she, and those like her, expect everyone to see and feel the offering of love that she brings. **Fore, it is – the highest goal or aspiration of your species to get outside of yourselves and assist your others.** Although, know that Coretta is at a higher spiritual and mental vibration than most on Earth. Coretta's Soul Plan and the Soul Plans of those like her ensure many things. They ensure that the very way and ways that she and they move, eat and act, is a catalyst for others to react and respond to her with love. She has a wonderful gift for all. Coretta, also, has within her Soul Plan the **ability to display** - the full spectrum of human emotions, at any given moment, for all to witness and adjust to. Coretta and those like her fully understand that the institutions that have and are being created for those like her, that most of you think are to help them deal with life and society, WE tell you, are exactly the other way around. The institutions have been created to help all others see the God or US in those that are considered autistic. Their gifts, which include their behaviors, are for the mothers, fathers, siblings, grandparents, friends and all of humanity. WE say to thee, Coretta has been instrumental in assisting your species. Coretta has helped in and with the understanding, finally, that she and those like her are not to be and should never be institutionalized. They are to be loved, cared for and respected. Yes, Coretta has a very special Soul Plan because she is an extraordinary human being.

A. – WE will just use this initial, for she is known worldwide as a comforter to the souls of many on Earth. In A's Soul Plan was for her to be a Spiritual Singer. A has the ability to sing at a very high-pitched octave with a full range of harmonic sounds. She has always had this ability. Her voice meshes with the very sounds of the Crystal Bowls that WE and you on Earth have created to calm the human soul. WE tell you, it is in her Soul Plan to make such melodic sounds. **She was given this gift from the Angelic Realm** upon leaving the Library of Souls, after reading her Book of Life prior to returning to your planet. And there are a few of you reading these very words that have the same gift or Soul Plan too. The question is – Will you use your gift or keep it to yourself? It was not, WE tell you, meant to be hidden.

Danny Q. – In Danny's Soul Plan was to Fight in Vietnam, lose both Legs and Never Walk Again. WE have changed the name of the encasement that WE speak of now. WE have done so out of what you may term as anonymity. Anyway, WE were doing a Private Session with Danny in Wisconsin. Danny had been very angry for a long time. He never told anyone how angry he really was. He questioned US many a day and night as to why this loss of limb would happen to him, yet WE never gave him an answer: it was not time. He even thought, for a long time, that he was abandoned by US. WE thanked him many a day during his quiet time for showing a brave face since the bomb blew his legs off. However, he did not hear. WE thanked him in a private session for helping other veterans to accept a like or similar situation in their lives. WE informed him that WE were going to tell him why it happened to him after only being in country (Vietnam) for only one week. WE informed him that it was a part of his Soul Plan. He looked at Elliott, as WE spoke to him through Elliott, with a dazed look. WE knew he was puzzled – don't forget there is nothing that WE do not know! Then WE informed him it was what he chose and created to occur since the day he was born; that he decided, before he ever entered his mother's belly, that one day he would lose his legs, help many, but not totally accept that which had occurred to him until WE spoke with him in a human voice. WE, further, informed him that it was his gift to humanity. His gift was the gift of compassion to all whom saw his face and heard his voice. Danny broke down in tears. Danny wept in that office and WE comforted him in the arms of Elliott. He stated, "Now I understand!" WE told him to go forth and remember that he is a gift to all, to hold his head up high and be proud of himself for fulfilling his Soul Plan.

Erwin M.— Erwin was born a soft soul. He, from the day he could understand, knew he had the Gift of Healing. This gift was in his Soul Plan, he fought it for almost fifty years. Then one day he surrendered and took a course on touch healing. Today he is a master, teaching others. Many things went on in his life prior to him becoming a master. Guess what? None of it matters. Fore, he changed his course and so can you.

Now WE could go on and on and on with billions of cases, yet WE won't. You should be beginning to get the point. You can pick up on your Soul Plan at any given point in your life. This is the only thing that matters in your life on Earth. It is the most important part of your very existence.

It's There Right In Front of You

It is right there.
Can't you see it?
It is literally right in front of you.
You can grab it now.
Don't let it get away.
It's right there. Get it!
Don't let it slip away.
It's over there.
Go get it. Can't you see it?
We see it, they see it.
What's wrong with you?
It's right in front of you.

Chapter 11

How to Find Your Life Plan & Map

Each of You

Each one of you has a Soul Plan. Your very life has great reason and purpose. WE tell you this, fore, it is true. However, for you to remember your Soul Plan, you **must** take care of self. Therefore, WE desire for all of you to be selfish, yet not in the classic sense or by the definition that most of you have been told.

> - To be devoted to only yourself or primarily to only be concerned with only your interests, regardless of the feelings and outcomes of your others.

No, this is not what WE mean.

**WE mean for you to truly care for self.

Therefore, once again WE reiterate:

1. Pray each day to US out loud, it is the only way to pray, sound and vibration. Anyone who told you anything else is mis-informed and has bought into the misinformation. Now, during quiet time or what you may think is meditation, one can send mental thoughts of hopes, desires and dreams to US. However, that is not meditation.

2. Meditate daily. **Meditation is silence.** Pure silence, being with US, not talking, no music, no sound generated by you except for the beat of your heart. And, no sound generated by anyone for you. The natural sounds around you, be it inside or outside, is **ALL YOU NEED for Meditation.** Once one has music or following what they perceive to be a guided meditation by a person's voice, or other sounds made specifically to calm the being, it is **Relaxation not Meditation.** During the appropriate meditation you can gain access to your Soul Plan given to you from the High Angelic.

3. You may also obtain information on your Soul Plan, Purposes and Life Map from a high vibrational Angel communicator or what you call a medium. However, once again, they must be of a high vibration. You can tell if they are at a high vibration through your own intuition and your vision. Someone at a high vibration will be generally **healthy, not excessively overweight. You are able to discern this. Additionally, you will be able to feel if they are at a high vibration and the eyes will be clear and draw you into them.**
4. Take the vitamins and supplements for your height, weight and skeletal frame. A good Naturopath, or communicator with Angels, High portions of US, or a pure Channeler of US will be able to let you know what you need.
5. Eat less meat. You do not have to cease eating meat if you do not desire to. Yet, it is in the best interest of your species to eat small portions of such.

6. Exercise. All of you need to do this. All of you need a certain amount of cardio that is more than a mere walk or stroll from time to time.
7. Seek out and find higher vibrational information. How will you know if it is of a high vibration? Good question. If it speaks of love and light, and if it does not say that the information is a secret, it is of a high vibration. Remember, high vibrational information is for all, not a select few. WE would not do that. If it includes in it the untruthful information about communicating with the dead, it is not of a high vibration. Only for certain reasons, that WE have laid out previously, about communication with a deceased loved one or a spirit that has left physical form is possible. Anyone whom informs you differently is lying to you. Now, it may not be on purpose. In most cases, it is simply due to the acceptance of mis-information.
8. Acquire some Stones and Crystals. They help to raise the human vibration.

9. Ask US for information into your Soul's Purpose. WE will answer you.

When you do the above listed routinely and consistently, **you will** lift your personal vibration and you will be able to complete your Soul Plan. Fore, you will be better able to assist others. You will begin to walk a spiritually high path. Old ideas will slip away, you will meditate, you will pray, you will exercise, you will eat less meat if any. And if you choose to not eat meat, **you will not judge those whom choose to continue to**, fore, it is acceptable. You will begin to understand things on a deeper level, you will stop protesting and start raising your own vibration, which will affect the entire matrix of your planet. You will study stones and begin to explore true spiritual ideas. You will become humble. You will laugh. You will cry. You will apologize, you will stop going against the current, fore, you are not the salmon. You are a spirit/soul having a human experience. You will know that you are light and love. You will understand that you matter. You will send all lower vibrations away from your being whenever and wherever they may appear. You will begin to teach, heal yourself, and assist others in doing the same. You will understand that everything in your life has brought you to where you are now. You will be grateful, thankful, a messenger of OURS. You will be fulling your Soul's Purpose and Plan.

Because you live on Earth, the **trick** is to make high vibrational decisions. This can only be accomplished by taking care of all aspects of the fourfold being. If proper care of self, which includes meditation, is actively engaged daily, the encasement will obtain the vibrational level necessary to know and fulfill its Soul Plan.

WE Love You So Very Much!

Shenanigan

The soul plan is no shenanigan.
There are no rascals trying to fool you,
Or trick you into following your spirit.
If you follow it, your life will not
Be placed in chaos, turmoil or upheaval.
Following it will make sure that you don't have to
Estimate or guess-timate, what to do.
All you have to do is follow,
High vibrational information.
Information that will not lead you,
Into a cult-like situation,
And bring about mental and emotional irritation,
Or subject you to proving your worth.
It will only bring up a new spiritual birth.

No, the soul plan is no shenanigan.
It is a spiritual safeguard,
To ensure that you won't falter,
And keep you from repeatedly
Going down the marriage altar.
The soul plan is a provision so,
You won't have to live again,

Or follow the road paved,
With the lie about sin again.
The soul plan is nothing more,
Than your best friend.
There are no basements to venture in.
No hidden chests to find.
There is no darkroom to develop in.

Your soul plan is no shenanigan.
All you have to do is follow the light,
The light of self, that leads to God,
So, your life can take flight.
All you have to do is follow,
The light of God that leads back to self.

Therefore, We suggest you place,
Your false pride and ego on the shelf,
So, you may find your natural self,
And come to fully understand,
That your soul plan is no shenanigan.

Keep up with Elliott & Diane:

Fb

From God to You: Absolute Truth and

Elliott Eli Jackson

****

Twitter

Elliott Eli Jackson

@IAmYouAreWEAre

****

Instagram – iamelliott1

****

www.quantummatrixcenter.com

Watch our videos

YouTube – ELLIOTTDIANE1

Made in the USA
Las Vegas, NV
01 March 2021